THE FRONTIER FORT

STIRRING TIMES IN THE NORTH-WEST TERRITORY OF BRITISH AMERICA

W. H. G. KINGSTON

1ST WORLD LIBRARY
Literary Society

The Frontier Fort

W. H. G. Kingston

© 1st World Library, 2007
PO Box 2211
Fairfield, IA 52556
www.1stworldlibrary.com
First Edition

LCCN: 2007934212

Softcover ISBN: 978-1-4218-9684-7
Hardcover ISBN: 978-1-4218-9784-4
eBook ISBN: 978-1-4218-9584-0

Purchase *"The Frontier Fort"*
as a traditional bound book at:
www.1stWorldLibrary.com/purchase.asp?ISBN=978-1-4218-9684-7

1st World Library is a literary, educational organization
dedicated to:

- Creating a free internet library of downloadable ebooks

- Hosting writing competitions and offering book publishing
scholarships.

Interested in more 1st World Library books? contact:
literacy@1stworldlibrary.com
Check us out at: www.1stworldlibrary.com

1st World Library Literary Society

Giving Back to the World

"If you want to work on the core problem, it's early school literacy."

- James Barksdale, former CEO of Netscape

"No skill is more crucial to the future of a child, or to a democratic and prosperous society, than literacy."

- Los Angeles Times

"Literacy... means far more than learning how to read and write... The aim is to transmit... knowledge and promote social participation."

- UNESCO

"Literacy is not a luxury, it is a right and a responsibility. If our world is to meet the challenges of the twenty-first century we must harness the energy and creativity of all our citizens."

- President Bill Clinton

"Parents should be encouraged to read to their children, and teachers should be equipped with all available techniques for teaching literacy, so the varying needs and capacities of individual kids can be taken into account."

- Hugh Mackay

CHAPTER ONE

A party of travellers were wending their way across a wide-spreading prairie in the north-west territory of America. As far as the eye could reach, the ground was covered with waving tufts of dark-green grass, interspersed with flowers of varied hue, among which could be distinguished the yellow marigold and lilac bergamot, with bluebells, hare-bells, and asters, innumerable; while here and there rose-bushes, covered with gorgeous bloom, appeared above the particoloured carpet spread over the country. On the north side the prairie was bounded by softly rounded knolls, between which tiny lakelets were visible, shining in the bright rays of the glowing sun. To the northward a silvery stream could be seen meandering, bordered by willows, aspens, osiers, and other trees of considerable height, breaking the line of the horizon.

"I am delighted with your country, Burnett; I had no idea such lovely scenery and so much rich soil existed on this side of the Rocky Mountains," said one of the travellers, addressing another, who rode alongside him.

"I hope, before many years are over, to see this fair region covered with populous towns and villages, and flourishing farms."

"That time is far distant, I suspect," answered Mr Burnett, a head clerk of the Hudson's Bay Company, in charge of the party; "and I can only say that I hope so, for when it comes, our vocation will be well-nigh gone, as the Company will have to shut up shop—"

"And retire on well-won fortunes," laughingly added the first speaker, Reginald Loraine. He was a young Englishman of good fortune and family, who had lately come out to make a tour in Canada; but having heard conflicting reports of the north-west territory, he had been induced to continue his journey westward, intending to proceed as far as the foot of the Rocky Mountains, and to return, before the termination of the summer, from Fort Edmonton, down the Saskatchewan, and through Lake Winnipeg to the Red River.

His intelligence, high spirits, and good humour made him an agreeable companion. He was never put out by any mishaps or inconveniences. His personal appearance was also much in his favour; while he was a good rider, and possessed of activity and endurance, equal, if not superior, to any of the rest of the party, long accustomed though they were to the mode of life they were leading.

From the sentiments he uttered, and the expression of his handsome countenance, it might have been surmised that he possessed many other qualities of a higher character. Young Hector Mackintosh, who had come with him from Toronto, declared, indeed, that he never wished to have a stauncher fellow at his back in a skirmish with Redskins, or in a fight with a grizzly, and that he was as high-minded and generous as he was brave.

Hector, who was now curvetting over the prairie on a tough little mustang, had been at school at Toronto, whence he was returning to rejoin his father, Captain Mackintosh, now a

W. H. G. Kingston

chief officer, or factor, in charge of Fort Duncan, a Company's post to the south-west, situated on the borders of the Blackfeet territory. It was a somewhat dangerous position, which only a man of courage and resolution would willingly have occupied.

Following at some little distance those who have been mentioned, came three other horsemen, whose shouts of laughter, interspersed occasionally with snatches of songs, could be heard far across the prairie. The centre of the three was a short, portly gentleman, with a somewhat rubicund countenance—Doctor McCrab, just appointed surgeon to one of the forts in the west. On either side of him rode two young clerks. One of them was Dan Maloney, a light-hearted Irishman, with whom the jolly Doctor amused himself by exchanging jokes, capping verses, and singing duets which set all the laws of harmony at defiance.

The other was Allan Keith, who, from similarity of taste and mental qualities, had won the regard of Reginald Loraine; indeed, except in point of wealth, the two young men greatly resembled each other.

Some way behind the gentlemen came a long team of Red River wooden carts, escorted by several persons on horse-back, under charge of Jacques Leblanc, a French half-breed, who, from his reputed knowledge of the country in all directions, had been selected to act as guide to the whole party.

The carts, which had only two wheels, were built entirely of wood, and each was dragged by a single horse. Some carried the travellers' tents, cooking utensils, a tool-chest, and additional axletrees, their arms and ammunition, together with their clothes, spare blankets, and waterproofs. The other carts were laden with stores of all sorts for the forts to the westward.

Accompanying the carts was a drove of loose horses—the animals now rearing and kicking and biting at each other—now moving along steadily, under the management of a single driver, Francois Chabot, also a French half-breed. He had seldom to use his long whip to keep them in order; and even the most restless showed no inclination to leave their companions. They were intended to supply the travellers with a change of steeds once or twice in the day; for in making long journeys, when day after day forty or fifty miles have to be got over between sunrise and sunset, one horse seldom possesses sufficient strength and endurance to carry his rider the whole distance.

When a horse shows signs of fatigue, his saddle is removed to the back of another, and he contentedly runs on with the herd. The horses were mostly small, and many of them sorry-looking steeds; but they had, notwithstanding, carried their riders without showing signs of fatigue, or growing thinner. Their only food was the grass they could pick up while the party were encamped at night, or during their noon-day halt, neither beans nor corn being given them.

Reginald Loraine and the Doctor had provided themselves with English saddles; the rest of the party bestrode those of native manufacture, which were merely large pads of dressed leather, stuffed with hair or grass, and having a broad and fringed crupper. Several of them were trimmed and handsomely adorned with quills, the talent of the manufacturer being especially exerted in ornamenting the saddle-cloths. The stirrups were formed of curved pieces of wood, hanging by leather thongs to the primitive saddle. The bridles might more properly be called halters. They consisted of a thong of raw hide, thirty feet in length, called an *atscacha*. One end was tied round the animal's lower jaw, and the other, after being brought over the neck to the rider's hand, was allowed to drag on the ground some fifteen feet behind. It requires care, particularly by those in the rear, not to tread on the thongs trailing behind. By so doing, the mouth of the horse receives a jerk which seldom fails to make it rear and curvet from side to side.

The object of this long thong is to enable the rider, when he dismounts, to hold his horse while he fires at a foe; or, should he be thrown by the animal stumbling in a rabbit-burrow, to prevent it running off. The long thong serves also as a halter, ever ready to tie it up, or to catch it when at liberty. Even the gentlemen who used English bridles found it convenient to have these halters secured to their horses' heads.

Day after day the travellers had been making their way along the Fertile Belt, the name given to a broad tract of country extending between the Red River and the base of the Rocky Mountains, bordered on the north by forests, lakes, and rivers, and on the south by that sandy and desert region which extends along the whole frontier of the United States.

The party rode steadily on, every man carrying his rifle at his back; for although the natives were generally friendly, it was considered wise to be prepared, lest so rich a booty as the carts would afford might tempt them. At night, too, a constant watch was kept on the horses, as the Crees roaming over that part of the country are notorious horse-stealers, and would have considered it a creditable feat to have carried off as many of the travellers' steeds as they could catch.

They had proceeded some distance, when, shading his eyes with his hand, Mr Burnett looked out eagerly ahead.

"What is it you see?" asked Loraine, imitating his example.

"A party of horsemen, whom I at first thought might be

Blackfeet on the war-path, but I am satisfied they are Red River men, on a buffalo hunt," answered Burnett. "We shall soon know. See, Leblanc has gone forward to ascertain who they are."

The guide in a short time returned, saying that the strangers were Red River hunters; that they had just sighted buffalo, and would be glad if any of the gentlemen of the party would join them.

Loraine and Hector were delighted to accept the invitation, and Allan Keith and Maloney were anxious to try their skill as hunters. While they galloped on to join the half-breeds, Burnett and his men moved towards the spot which had been fixed on for camping at night.

The buffalo hunt need not be described, except to say that the young Englishmen won the admiration of their new friends by their courage and dexterity, each having brought a couple of the shaggy monsters to the ground.

The travellers spent the evening with their new friends, the hunters, who, as soon as the buffalo they had last killed had been turned into pemmican, intended to return to the Red River. Next morning they continued their journey westward, pushing on at greater speed than usual, to make up for lost time, Burnett being very anxious to reach the fort by the day he was expected.

The country was generally lovely, being well wooded, with numerous lakelets, now rising into softly rounded knolls, and occasionally opening out into a wide, fair landscape. The soil was of rich loam, and the vegetation luxuriant, sprinkled with flowers of many tints.

They had been moving on for a couple of hours or more,

when Loraine, looking to the southward, observed a remarkable appearance in the horizon, which wore an unearthly ashen hue. Pointing it out to Burnett, he asked—

"Can that be produced by a prairie fire?"

"No; but if I mistake not, we shall have, before long, a flight of locusts passing over our heads. That peculiar look of the sky is produced by the light reflected from their transparent wings."

As he spoke, the whole sky appeared to be changing from blue to silvery white, then to ashy grey and lead colour; while, opposite to the sun, the prevailing hue was a silver white—perceptibly flashing, the air seeming as if filled with flakes of snow.

"The insects are flying from five hundred to a thousand feet above our heads; and I hope we may get clear of them before we camp, or they will play mischief with everything made of leather, which is left exposed," observed Burnett.

He was, however, disappointed; for, in a short time, the locusts descended—the whole air became filled with them, until they reached the ground, where they clung to the blades of grass in countless multitudes.

During the remainder of the day the creatures continued coming on; and when the party at length stopped at night, they had to clear away the ground to form their camp.

The voracity of the insects was proved by the way they attacked and destroyed several articles of clothing, which had carelessly been left on the grass. The travellers found, indeed, that the only way to protect their property was to pile it up in the carts out of reach. Dan Maloney appeared with a melancholy countenance, exhibiting a leather bag and a pair of woollen trousers, which he had thrown down outside the tent, eaten through and through in all directions. At night the insects, fortunately, did not move. Early in the morning they were found busily feeding; but as soon as the sun had evaporated the dew, they began taking short flights, and then cloud after cloud rose, and pursued their way to the northward.

Burnett assured his companions that he had never seen so large a flight before; and, as far as he could ascertain, many years had passed without the country receiving a similar visitation.

Scarcely had the locusts disappeared, than what looked like a thick, black fog-bank was seen rising from the direction whence they had come. It approached nearer and nearer. Leblanc, riding forward, pointed it out to Burnett.

"The prairie is on fire," he remarked.

"I know it is; I saw it from the first. But I don't think it will come near us."

"I am not quite so sure of that. It comes on fast, and the grass here is very long," said the guide.

"Then we'll make our way to yonder knoll, where it is shorter," said Burnett, who was not to be put out by Indians, locusts, or prairie fires.

The word was given to drag the carts towards the spot Burnett had indicated.

"A fire on the prairie is a serious matter, is it not?" observed Loraine, in a tone of inquiry.

"I do not much fear it, notwithstanding," answered Burnett. "We shall have a storm before long, I suspect, and that will fight the flames."

"I should have thought that a storm would be more likely to fan them into greater fury," remarked Loraine, who considered that Burnett was not sufficiently alive to the dangers they might have to encounter from the fire.

"Not if it rains as I expect it will," observed Burnett. "Look at that cloud ahead. It contains a torrent sufficient to extinguish the fiercest flames."

Loraine had hitherto been admiring the beautiful appearance of the sky. To the south it was of that bright blue such as is seldom seen in the British Isles. To the west it was bordered with vast, billowy clouds of the softest, snowy white. Beneath the black cloud, which was every instant extending, were grey masses whirling on at a terrific rate; while, suddenly, to the north and east the expanse of heaven assumed a dun-coloured hue, vivid with lightning, where rain appeared to be descending in torrents. The whole atmosphere was charged with electricity. The lightning rushed towards the earth, in straight and zig-zag currents, the thunder varying from the sharp rattle of musketry to the roar of artillery. Still no rain had fallen from overhead, while scarcely a breath of air was blowing.

Meantime, however, the fire came rushing on across the prairie, the flames, as they caught the tall grass, growing brighter and brighter, every now and then rising and expanding, as they seized on shrubs and trees in their onward course.

Burnett at last seemed to think that matters were growing serious, and made a signal to the drivers of the carts to push forward. There was no necessity, as they were doing their utmost to urge on their steeds by uttering strange oaths and by the liberal use of their whips.

"We must try and get to the other side of the knoll, and camp; for we as yet have only seen the beginning of the storm," remarked Burnett.

Scarcely had he said this, than, with the suddenness of a tornado, the wind came rushing down upon them; at first, without a drop of rain, but so fiercely that the horses were forced from the track. Again and again it seemed hopeless to drive against it. The lightning flashed more vividly than before; the thunder roared; while the fire advanced across the prairie like a fiery host bent on their destruction.

"I say, I don't see why we should lose our lives, even though Burnett thinks it is his duty to stick by the carts," said Hector, riding up to Loraine. "We can gallop ahead, in spite of the wind; it will be better than being turned into Guy Fawkeses."

Loraine was much inclined to follow his young friend's advice; indeed, he suspected the rest of the party would soon leave the carts to their fates, and try to save themselves by flight from the fiery sea, which was tossing and heaving not a quarter of a mile away from them. He would not go, however, without first urging Burnett, the other clerks, and the Doctor to try and save themselves.

He had turned his horse for the purpose, when the rain came down thick and furious, with even greater suddenness than the wind had arisen. They saw that it almost immediately produced an effect on the fire. It was a struggle between the two elements. At first it seemed doubtful, however, which would prove victorious; but water, they trusted, had gained

W. H. G. Kingston

the day; for, mingled with the rain came hail, not only ordinary hail, but mixed with lumps half an inch to an inch across.

"Och! I'd as soon have a whack from an honest shillaly as be pelted by thim threacherous lumps," cried Dan Maloney.

The travellers in vain raised their hands to protect their heads from the hail. The long line of horses and carts was broken. Some of the poor creatures clung to the road, struggling desperately. Others were driven on to the prairie, and turning their backs to the storm, stood still or moved sideways, with cowering heads, their manes and tails floating wildly, like those of Highland shelties.

Hector declared that he could hear the hissing of the rain as it fell on the hitherto victorious fire, effectually, however, quenching it. A few minutes after the storm had broken, the whole ground to the left was a blackened expanse. The danger was passed, and they hastened on to the foot of the knoll, where a lakelet, fringed by aspens and poplars, afforded them good camping ground. With astonishing speed the arrangements for the night were made; every man exerted himself. The horses were unharnessed, the erratic ones hobbled, the tents pitched, and the travellers assembled round the blazing fires which were quickly lighted to dry their saturated clothing.

Almost before these arrangements were made, the storm passed away. The setting sun burst forth again until not a blot was left in the sky, save fragments of mist to the south and south-east. It was too late to think of moving on again, and Leblanc was glad of the opportunity of halting to repair some of the carts with the ever serviceable "Shaganappi," a large supply of which was carried for the purpose, as also to mend the harness and other gear which had been broken by the restive movements of the horses during the storm.

In the mean time, while Francois, another Canadian, who acted as cook, was preparing the evening meal, Loraine and Hector took their guns to shoot some ducks which were seen on the other side of the lakelet. Having knocked over several birds, before returning they took a refreshing plunge in the water, which was sufficiently deep for the purpose.

The twilight had faded away into darkness before the whole party were seated round the camp-fires, discussing their suppers with such appetites as few fail to obtain while travelling in that region. Supper was over; and "early to bed, and early to rise" being a standing order, those of the party who enjoyed the luxury of tents retired within, while the rest lay down, wrapped in their blankets, beneath the carts arranged, as usual, in a circle to serve as a defence against any attacks of hostile Indians. Although Burnett did not expect any annoyance of the sort, he considered it his duty to take the precautions which no traveller at that period omitted to make. Two or three men were also stationed as sentries to keep watch, especially on the horses.

Loraine had seen Hector, who shared his tent, fall fast asleep; but not being inclined to close his own eyes, he stepped out of his tent to take a look at the stars which shone from the heavens, undimmed by a single cloud. Happening to turn his eyes towards the summit of the knoll, he was somewhat surprised to see what he felt sure was a human figure, the outline being distinctly marked against the sky. The man was evidently taking a survey of the camp. Loraine, thinking it possible that he might be a scout sent out by a party of Blackfeet, made his way to the nearest sentry to tell him to be on the watch, and to ask his opinion on the subject. By the time he had reached the sentry, however, the figure had disappeared. The sentry thought he might have been mistaken; but when Loraine made him understand what he had seen, he went round to the other men on watch, and urged them to be on the alert and to keep the horses well together. Loraine was just going back to his tent, when he heard a shout. It was answered by the sentry on the south side of the camp; and a conversation in a language he could not understand took place. On going up to them, he could dimly distinguish an Indian of somewhat diminutive size and of deformed figure.

"What does he want?" inquired Loraine.

"He says, as far as I can make out, that his chief, who will be here directly, sent him to find out who we are; for he thought at first, when he saw our camp-fire, that we might be Crees. or a party of Blackfeet, for such he knows are at present out on the war-path," answered the sentry.

"Tell him that we shall be glad to see his chief, whoever he is, if he comes as a friend," said Loraine. "Until I know his business, I will not arouse Mr Burnett, who requires a good rest; and I dare say it will keep until to-morrow morning."

The sentry spoke to the hump-backed Indian, who quickly disappeared in the gloom; and Loraine walked up and down, waiting for his return.

"You must not be thrown off your guard, Pierre, lest some trick should be intended," he remarked, recollecting the numberless tales of Indian treachery he had heard.

"I know the coquins (rogues) too well for that," answered Pierre.

In a short time, Loraine saw through the gloom two persons on horseback, with a couple of led horses, approaching. They rode fearlessly up to the camp. The first, from the white hair hanging down under his fur cap, and his snowy beard, and wrinkled, weather-beaten features, though he sat upright and firmly in his saddle, was apparently an old man. His costume, consisting of a leathern coat and leggings, fringed in the usual fashion, and the rifle slung at his back, showed that he was one of the free white hunters, or trappers, who have been wont for many a year to roam amid the prairies and forests in the north-west in search of peltries. The other person, leading the two pack horses, Loraine recognised as the hump-backed Indian who had just before come to the camp.

"I am glad to have fallen in with you, friends," said the old man, dismounting. "You keep early hours and a careful watch. I expected to have seen you carousing, and quaffing the accursed fire-water, as so many of you travellers from the Far East are wont to do. To say the truth, when I first caught sight of your camp-fires, I was uncertain whether they were those of Crees or Blackfeet; and as I had no fancy to fall in with the one or the other, I sent on my lad Greensnake to learn the state of the case."

"Then he was the person I saw at the top of the hillock out there," observed Loraine.

"Not he; he would not have exposed himself in that fashion," said the old man.

"Then my eyes must have deceived me, after all," said Loraine. "I'm sure Mr Burnett, the leader of our party, will welcome you to the camp; but he is asleep at present, and I should be sorry to disturb him unnecessarily. I will, however, call up one of the men to get ready some supper for you and your attendant."

"I shall be glad of some food, for I have not fired a shot for the last three days, and my stock of provisions has run short," replied the old man.

He now called up Greensnake, took off the saddles from the led horses, and unloaded the baggage animals, placing the packs inside the circle of carts.

Meantime, Loraine found out where Francois was sleeping, and, arousing him, told him to get some food ready for their unexpected guests.

Francois at first eyed the strangers askance. Satisfied, however, at length, that he was a white man, and perhaps a person of more importance than his costume might betoken, he set diligently to work to boil the kettle and fry some buffalo meat; the old hunter, who had taken a seat on a pile of wood near the fire, looking complacently on.

Loraine having assisted Francois in preparing the supper, prompted by good feeling, and perhaps slightly by curiosity, took a seat by the side of the stranger, that he might attend to his wants. Immediately afterwards, the lad who has been introduced as Greensnake glided noiselessly up in a fashion appropriate to his name, and squatted down close to his master, waiting patiently until Loraine handed him a share of the food. Having no cause to conceal the object of their journey, Loraine explained that he and his companions were bound for Fort Edmonton, and were pushing on as fast as they could travel, without the risk of knocking up their horses.

"I wish that you were directing your course rather to Fort Duncan, for I suspect that Captain Mackintosh and his small garrison are greatly in want of assistance. From some information brought me by Greensnake, I suspect that the

Blackfeet have formed a plot to take it. Hearing that the Captain holds the Indians cheaply, and is not likely to be warned by what I might tell him, I am on my way to Fort Edmonton to advise that he should be put on his guard, and that assistance may be sent him without delay."

Loraine was struck by the old man's mode of expressing himself—so different to the slang language used in general by the rough trappers and traders of the Far West.

"This is important information, indeed!" he said, feeling anxious about the safety of his young friend's family, and especially of that young friend's two sisters; for although he had never seen them, Hector had shown him their portraits, one of which, called Sybil, possessed a face of rare loveliness. Effie, the younger, was very attractive; but Hector declared that there never was, or never could be, anybody like Sybil. Hector had told him that the portrait, not being his own, he could not give it to him, but that he was welcome to look at it as often as he liked—a privilege of which, it must be confessed, Reginald frequently took advantage; and he had resolved, if possible, to pay a visit to the residence of the fair original. Even had this not been the case, his chivalry would have made him eager to set off to the assistance of Hector's relatives. He felt that the matter was of so much importance that he should be justified in calling up Mr Burnett to discuss what measures should be taken. He, of course, knew that Hector would be as anxious to go as he was; he, therefore, let him sleep on. Burnett, who did not appear very well satisfied at being aroused from his slumbers, came and sat down to hear the old man's account. He questioned him narrowly, apparently not altogether crediting his statements.

"You may think what you will, Mr Burnett; but people are not apt in general to doubt the word of Isaac Sass," said the old man at length, in an offended tone.

"Are you Isaac Sass?" exclaimed Burnett. "I have often heard of you. Then, I say, I don't doubt your word. But why are you so sure that the fort will be attacked?"

"For a strong reason, which, as I don't wish to keep you longer from your rest, I will give in the morning."

"A word for yourself, friend Sass, I ken?" observed Burnett.

"No, no; I can do without sleep," answered Isaac Sass; "but before I lie down, I wish to know—yes or no—whether you will direct your course towards Fort Duncan, instead of going on to Edmonton."

"I wish that I could do as you suggest," answered Burnett. "If Captain Mackintosh wants help, I should like to give it him; but I must carry out my instructions, at all costs. It would not do to run the risk of getting our train plundered, as both stores and ammunition are much wanted at Edmonton."

"But will you allow one of your factors to be exposed to the danger our friend here has spoken of?" exclaimed Loraine. "I should be unwilling under any other circumstances to part company; but I feel bound, whether or not I can get anybody to go with me, to set off with my friend, young Mackintosh, to warn his family, and give them such assistance as we can."

"You, of course, are at liberty to go, Mr Loraine; and, as young Mackintosh was committed to your care, to take him with you," answered Burnett, somewhat stiffly. "But duty is duty. I must obey my orders, and those are, to conduct this train to Edmonton with as little delay as possible. I have no discretionary power to go out of the way, under any excuse whatever."

"But, surely, you would not object to one of the clerks, and some few of the men who could be spared, accompanying me!" exclaimed Loraine. "Even a small addition to the number would be of consequence in the defence of the fort, should it be attacked; and that it will be so, our friend here seems to think there is every probability."

"I have explained how I am situated in the matter, Mr Loraine," said Mr Burnett, in the same tone as before; "and I think it right to say, that, without a guide and a body of men well-armed, you and young Mackintosh will be unable to accomplish the journey. You will either lose yourselves and be starved, or be attacked and cut off by the Blackfeet. The Crees are not to be trusted either; for though they are civil enough to us, knowing that we have the power to punish them, yet they would steal our horses if they could; and, looking upon you as strangers, they would not only take your horses, but your scalps into the bargain."

"I shall not be afraid of meeting either them or the Black-feet," answered Loraine. "What do you say, friend?" he added, turning to Isaac Sass. "Can I, or can I not, get to Fort Duncan, and warn the garrison of the danger which threatens them?"

The old hunter looked up at the countenance of the young Englishman, without speaking for a few seconds. He then said, "If pluck and courage would enable a man to do it, you would; but I cannot say how much you know about the country and the ways of the Redskins. It would not be an easy matter for any man, as there are several war parties out—of that I have certain knowledge; and I had no small difficulty in keeping clear of them. I wish that I could go with you, but I cannot get along as fast as I used to do, and my beasts are pretty well knocked up. But this is what I'll do: I'll send my lad Greensnake with you; whatever I tell him to do, he'll do, and prove as true as steel. People call him an idiot; but he's no more an idiot than I am, if a person knows how to get the sense out of him, and that's what I do."

Greensnake, on hearing his name mentioned, glanced up with a pleased look, and nodded at his master, as a dog often does when spoken about.

"I gladly accept your offer, and will give him any reward you think right for his services," said Loraine. "I should like to set off to-night."

"That would be impossible, as the lad and your horses want rest," answered the old trapper. "To-morrow morning he shall be at your service, and perhaps by that time Mr Burnett will have thought the matter over, and will send two or three of his men to accompany you. I will take the duties of those who go, and he knows I am worth something."

"Well, well, I'll think it over, and to-morrow morning let you know my decision," said Burnett. "Now, Mr Loraine, I'd advise you to lie down and get some rest, or you won't be fit for the work you propose to undertake."

Loraine, hoping that Burnett would consent to spare him a few men, followed his advice, and turned into his camp bed, while the old hunter, wrapping himself in his buffalo robe, lay down with his feet to the fire, as did Greensnake in a horse-cloth, which he took from the baggage he had deposited inside the camp.

CHAPTER TWO

Burnett was duly impressed with a sense of his responsibilities. He really wished to send assistance to Fort Duncan, but felt the importance of conveying his charge safely to Fort Edmonton, and he was too prudent to run any risk, by weakening his escort. He, therefore, determined to commence the journey at an earlier hour than usual, and to push forward as fast as possible. He recollected the half-breeds from whom they had parted only three days before, and whom they had left encamped. If they could be overtaken, some of them might be induced to go to Fort Duncan by the prospect of a brush with their sworn enemies, the Blackfeet. "Perhaps this young Englishman will agree to go back and obtain their assistance, and he will render far greater service to the captain than if he were to go alone," thought Burnett. "I will propose the plan to him to-morrow morning, and allow Allan Keith to accompany him. The two seem to pull well together; and as soon as we get to Edmonton we will send off as many men as can be spared."

Satisfied with his plan, Burnett pulled his blanket round him, and was just dropping off to sleep, when he heard the distant neigh of a horse.

"That was not one of our animals!" he exclaimed, starting to his feet. As he did so, he saw the old man and his Indian boy sitting up.

"What sound was that, Sass?" he asked.

"Blackfeet are not far off, I guess," was the answer.

Loraine, who had been unable to sleep, hearing what was said, came out of his tent.

"Is there a chance of the camp being attacked?" he asked.

"They'll not attack the camp, but they'll steal our horses if they can," answered Burnett.

"Depend on that; if we don't keep a look-out they'll have half of them away before morning," observed Sass; and turning to Loraine, he added, "You said just now that you caught sight of a figure on the top of the hill, and as that was not Greensnake or me, I have a notion that it was one of the Blackfeet."

"Why didn't you tell me of that before?" inquired Burnett.

"Because I thought I was mistaken, and that it was not of sufficient consequence to arouse you," answered Loraine.

"It may be of the greatest importance; even now the rascals may have enticed off some of our horses," exclaimed Burnett, taking his gun, and going up to where the men lay asleep.

A light touch on the shoulder, and a whisper in the ear, were sufficient to arouse them. He having also called up the Doctor and the two clerks, hurried on to where the men were on watch outside. They also had heard the sounds, and were on the alert. They were certain that as yet all the horses were safe. They were joined by most of the other men; two or three only, by Burnett's orders, having remained behind to extinguish the fires.

Just at this juncture several horses, feeding on the rich pasture not a hundred yards off, came galloping up, and would have passed the camp had not the men rushed out and stopped them. This proved without doubt that enemies were in the neighbourhood. Accordingly, several men, well-armed, went out and brought up the remainder of the horses, which they at once tethered either to the carts or to stakes firmly fixed in the ground; then each with his gun loaded with buck-shot, crawled out through the long grass, so that they could not be seen, even by the sharp eyes of the Blackfeet, and arranged themselves in a circle at the distance of about eighty yards from the camp. The night was dark, and perfect silence was maintained, so that even the most watchful enemy could not have discovered what the travellers were about.

Burnett having thus made all necessary arrangements for the security of the camp, directed Allan Keith and Maloney each to take his turn in watching, and again lay down, his example being followed by the rest of the party who were not required on duty. The most sharp-eyed Redskins would have found it difficult to discover what the travellers were about. Allan Keith was the only person who remained on foot. Having visited the horses, and ascertained that the men in charge of them were awake, he went on, intending to make the circuit of the camp, to assure himself that the men were on the alert. Thinking it unnecessary to crawl along the ground, from supposing that in the darkness he could not be seen at any distance, he walked upright, and had just got close to the outer circle where he expected to find one of the men on watch, when an arrow whistled close to his head. The scout, who must have been close in front of him, immediately began to crawl along, like a snake through the grass, in the direction whence the arrow had come.

Allan was as courageous as most persons; but it would have been folly to have exposed himself to the risk of another shot. He, therefore, wisely crouched down in the spot which had been occupied by the man who had gone forward in pursuit of the intruder. He listened with open ears, but not a sound could he hear, nor could his eyes pierce the darkness beyond a few yards from where he lay. He waited and waited, until he began to fear that the scout must have been caught by the savages, and killed before he had had time to cry out. That the other scouts were on the watch, he had no doubt, and would take care that no Indians approached without being discovered. He had remained in his recumbent position for some time, when he at length heard a rustling in the grass, and the scout rejoined him.

"The coquin has escaped us, monsieur," whispered the Canadian. "I wish that I had shot him, but by firing I should have discovered our position, and we should have had a score of arrows or bullets flying about our ears."

After the warning he had received, Allan, imitating the example of the scout, crawled along the ground to the different posts, and finding all the men on the alert, returned in the same fashion to the camp.

Night went by, and no other alarm was raised. At early dawn Burnett, having aroused the whole camp, gave them the information Isaac Sass had brought.

There was no lack of volunteers, among whom was Allan Keith, eager to accompany Loraine to Fort Duncan. He was somewhat less disappointed than would otherwise have been the case at being refused permission to go, when Burnett explained his plan of sending him in search of the half-breed hunters, to collect among them as many recruits as he could obtain to increase the garrison at Fort Duncan.

"I, at all events, will go with you!" exclaimed Hector, turning to Loraine. "We have a compass, and as I know the direction in which the fort lies, I shall not be afraid of missing my way."

"You forget the Redskins, and that you must be on your guard at night, or you'll have your horses stolen," observed old Sass. "You will also have to look out for game to support yourselves. However, if you take Greensnake with you, he'll help you to kill game, and will give due notice if enemies are near you."

"Yes, although I should have been glad to have had more companions, I am ready to set out at once," said Loraine.

"I am sorry I cannot spare any of my men," observed Burnett. "Two or three, indeed, would make but little difference, and the smaller your party the better for safety's sake. However, you must let your horses breakfast, for they got but little feeding last night, thanks to the Blackfeet."

While these and other arrangements were being made, the scouts came in. It was evident, they reported, from the tracks round the camp, that they had been surrounded by a large band, who would probably have stolen all their horses had they not been on their guard. The scouts, they added, had followed to a considerable distance the tracks which led away to the westward, and it was their opinion that the Indians would keep ahead, and not make another attempt to steal the horses till they fancied that the party were off their guard. It was so far satisfactory to have discovered the direction the Indians had taken, as Loraine might thus

W. H. G. Kingston

proceed southward and Allan Keith make his way eastward on the trail of the buffalo hunters, without the risk of encountering them.

"I will spare no exertion to get as soon as possible to the fort with as many men as I can induce to accompany me," said Allan, as he warmly shook hands with Loraine. "I heartily wish that I could have gone with you; but I must obey the orders of my chief. I am well acquainted with the family of Captain Mackintosh; pray give them my respects, and say how deeply I regret not being able to proceed at once to the fort."

Allan looked somewhat conscious as he said this. Loraine promised to deliver his messages; and the horses having now had time to feed, the three parties separated. Allan, accompanied by Pierre, rode off to the eastward; Mr Burnett and the train continued their journey to the west; while Loraine and his two companions took a southerly course.

"Good-bye, good-bye, my young friends," cried Dr McCrab, after riding a short distance with Loraine and Hector. "Whatever you do; don't let the Redskins take your scalps, my boys. Keep your powder dry, and your larder well stored, and you'll get through. I heartily wish that I could go with you; but I ride too heavy a weight, and should certainly delay you if we had to run for it with a pack of howling savages at our tails: the chances are, I should come off second best," said the good-natured medico, when, shaking hands, he turned his horse's head and galloped off to overtake the train brought up by Isaac Sass and his pack animals. The country being level, the train could be seen for a long distance, creeping on like a huge snake through the grass.

As Loraine looked round, a uniform and well-defined horizon met his eye. So destitute was the country in general of all landmarks, that he was thankful to have a good compass to guide his course, in addition to the assistance of the young hump-backed Indian, who depended on his instinct alone. Loraine and Hector had each a spare horse, which carried their changes of clothes, a store of powder and shot, and such provisions and cooking utensils as they were likely to require.

The young Indian frequently raised himself in his stirrups, and sometimes even stood upon the back of his horse, to take a look round, but dropped quickly down again into his saddle, satisfied that no foes were in the neighbourhood.

"It was fortunate that the Blackfeet came about the camp last night, and then took themselves off to the westward, as we are the less likely to have them on our trail," observed Hector, who was highly delighted to be able to go home at once, instead of having to make a long circuit, as he had expected, through Edmonton. Though he had heard the report of old Sass, he had not realised the danger in which his family might be placed.

He rattled on as was his wont, never failing to find subjects of conversation. "I did not suppose that there would be much risk, or I should not have proposed your coming with me," observed Loraine. "I was, besides, unwilling to make my appearance at the fort without you, lest Captain Mackintosh should look upon me as an impostor."

"I am very sure my father would not do that, or my mother or sister either, or Sybil. They'll make a good deal of you, I can tell you; for it is not often they see a gentleman at the fort, except Allan Keith, who comes whenever he can. He is, I suspect, a great admirer of my sister; and I am not surprised, for she is a dear, good girl, and worthy of the best fellow in the country."

"Which sister?" very naturally asked Loraine. "You showed me the portraits of two."

"I have only one. Sybil is not really my sister, though I called her so, and she is like a sister to us all. My father and mother adopted her before Effie or any of us were born; and as they were as fond of her as they could have been had she been their own child, she has lived on with us ever since. She's as pretty as she looks in her portrait, and as good and bright as she is pretty, and we boys love her as much as we do Effie."

This account naturally increased Loraine's desire to see the original of the beautiful picture; but a sense of delicacy prevented him further questioning his young companion about her, being well assured that he would before long tell him all he knew. Hector, indeed, talked away for the whole party, for Greensnake never uttered a word except from absolute necessity, and then it was in Cree. Hector, however, remembered enough to make out the meaning, having known the language before he went to school, and he translated what was said to Loraine. They had got to some distance from the camp, when Hector, turning round, observed two animals following.

"Holloa! What are these?" he exclaimed. "Can they be wolves?"

"If they are," said Loraine, "and they come near enough, we must shoot them, or they may interfere with our horses at night, especially as they are likely to pick up companions on the way."

"Very well; then we will stop at once, and do you fire at one of the brutes, and I will try to kill the other," said Hector. "What do you say, Greensnake?" he asked in Cree.

The hump-backed Indian grunted out an unintelligible reply, and pointed ahead.

"He doesn't think it worth while to stop," remarked Hector.

"Nor do I," said Loraine; and they accordingly pushed on at the pace they had before been going.

After a while, Hector, looking back, exclaimed, "Why, they are not wolves at all, but a couple of dogs—Old Buster, who belongs to the Doctor, and Dan Maloney's Muskey! They took a great fancy to me, for I used to play with them; but I had no idea of enticing them away from their masters."

"They must have found out that we are not with the train, and bolting, followed up our trail," remarked Loraine. "We cannot drive them back now."

The dogs were quickly up to the riders, and seemed highly delighted to find Hector, jumping up on either side of him.

The prairie which Loraine and his companions were traversing was almost treeless; but not many years before it had been covered with a pine forest, destroyed by one of the ruthless prairie fires which so often sweep over the north-west territory. Here and there, however, by the sides of streams, or pools, numerous aspens—the fastest growing trees in that region—had again sprung up, their stems being of considerable thickness, while their light foliage gave a cheerful aspect to the otherwise dreary scenery. When the ground allowed it, they occasionally put their horses into a gallop—a pace well suited to their tempers. At the same time, they knew that they must not run the risk of knocking up their animals, or they would fail in their object of making a quick journey.

They had gone on for some time, when Hector's tough little horse suddenly came down, and threw him over its head.

"Don't care for me," he cried; "but I'm afraid my horse has broken its leg."

The animal had put its foot into a badger-hole. After making some violent struggles, however, it recovered itself, and Hector, getting hold of its bridle, remounted.

"We must keep a better look-out for the badger-holes. It wouldn't be pleasant to have to continue our journey on foot," he said, laughing.

Having stopped by the side of a pool to take a mid-day meal, give their horses water, and allow them to crop as much grass as they could during the time, the travellers pushed on until nightfall, when they encamped under shelter of a grove of aspens, close to a stream, which flowed into the South Saskatchewan. By Greensnake's advice, only a small fire was lighted, which was to be put out when they had cooked their supper.

As soon as he had finished his meal, the Indian, taking his blanket, went and lay down close to where the horses which had been hobbled were feeding; while Loraine and Hector rolled themselves in their buffalo robes, leaving the two dogs to keep watch by their sides.

CHAPTER THREE

Fort Duncan, to which it is time the reader should be introduced, lay bathed in the ruddy glow of the setting sun, whose rays tinged the branches of the groves of aspen, birch, poplar, and spruce, which could be seen at some distance away, both to the east and west. It stood on the top of some high ground, rising abruptly from the margin of a stream flowing by on the north side.

The fort consisted of a square palisade, thirty feet or so in height, with rough wooden towers at each angle, connected by a narrow platform, which ran round inside the walls, a few feet below their summit. The only entrance was by a gate, flanked by two additional towers. This could be secured by strong bars, but was destitute of ditch, draw-bridge, or portcullis. The interior of the quadrangle was occupied by the residence of the chief factor and clerks, a hall used as an audience room, and a store-house, besides the dwellings of the hunters and their wives and children, and other persons forming the garrison. The land immediately round the fort had been cleared of trees; but there was a forest on one side, and scattered groups of timber on the other, affording abundance of wood for building purposes and fuel.

There was much beauty in the surrounding scenery, especially when the roses were in full bloom, and other flowers

W. H. G. Kingston

of varied hue enamelled the prairie. In a room of the fort, furnished with far more elegance than is generally seen in the north-west territory, sat two young ladies. Though both attractive, they differed greatly from each other. The youngest, of small figure, was fair, with light hair and blue, laughing eyes, her rosy mouth constantly wreathed in smiles. The elder was somewhat taller, of a richer colour, with dark brown hair, and was even more attractive in appearance than her companion. They were busily employed with their needles, talking in the mean time on some interesting subject, when their conversation was interrupted by the entrance of a fine lad, who, although a couple of years older, might have been known by his strong resemblance to be the brother of Hector Mackintosh.

"Come along, Sybil—come along, Effie—if you want to see a war-chief, thoroughly got up in his finest toggery," exclaimed Norman. "He is Mysticoose, or the Roaring Bull, not a very romantic name—a great leader among the Blackfeet. He has come to sell several packages of peltries and a whole lot of buffalo robes. He'll probably take his departure before long; so if you want to inspect him, you must come at once."

"Do you, Sybil, wish to see this savage chief?" asked Effie.

"By all means," answered Sybil. "I should like to make a sketch of him while he is bartering his peltries." And she took up a sketchbook and pencil from the table.

"Let me bring your paint-box," said Effie, "for you will make a much more interesting drawing if you colour it."

"I will try, if Norman will get a mug of water and hold it for me. We must not let the chief discover what we are about, or the poor savage may fancy we are bewitching him," said Sybil, laughing.

On going out of the house, they proceeded to the spot in front of the store where the trading business was transacted. Captain Mackintosh, a fine-looking man of middle age, and two of his clerks, stood on one side, a quantity of goods piled up near them; while on the other was seen an Indian chief, standing near several bales of peltries, and attended by a band of nearly twenty followers. His appearance was picturesque in the extreme. His head was adorned with a circlet of tall plumes. His dress consisted of a coat of dressed deer-skin, tastefully ornamented with beads and quill-work, as were his leggings, with long tassels, while a white wolf-skin cloak hung over one shoulder, and necklaces, composed of the teeth of bears and other animals, hung about his neck. He had been keenly bargaining with his host; but no sooner did the young ladies appear than he glanced towards them, his eyes wandering from one to the other, until they settled on Sybil with a look of evident admiration. She, however having begun her sketch, continued drawing, regarding the Indian much as if he had been a lay figure dressed up to copy.

Captain Mackintosh had at length to recall his attention to the matter they were engaged on. The assistants on each side continued to weigh the peltries, and hand over the articles given in exchange; but the young chief seemed to have lost all the interest he had previously shown, and instead of haggling as before over the price, made no objection to any of the goods offered him, which his attendants packed up as they received them, and carried out of the fort.

The trading being over, instead of following his people, the young chief advanced to Captain Mackintosh, and addressed him in a long speech, the meaning of which neither Sybil nor Effie could understand. Had they done so, they would have been very much surprised to find that Mysticoose was offering to make Sybil his wife, and to give in exchange for her, peltries and robes sufficient to fill the store-house of the fort. Captain Mackintosh answered, with due caution, that it was not the custom of English ladies to marry unless they could give their hearts to the persons who desired to possess them, nor that of fathers to receive payment; but that he would tell his daughter of the honour the chief intended her, although he would hold out no prospect that she would consent to quit her home, and become the bride of one whose people differed so much in their habits and customs, as well as in their religion, from his.

On this, Mysticoose declared that he would be ready to learn the religion of the pale-faces and adopt their customs, and entreated that he might be allowed the opportunity of declaring his sentiments to the maiden.

Captain Mackintosh, though very much annoyed, kept his countenance as well as his temper, and endeavoured to persuade the chief that he could find a far more suitable wife among his own people, with whose beauty he would be satisfied, and who would labour for him like her sisters in general. All he could say, however, did not appear to have any effect in turning the young chief from his purpose; but, on the contrary, he grew more and more eager, as if determined to succeed.

All the time Sybil, unconscious that she was the subject of conversation, went on with her sketch; and as she drew rapidly, she succeeded in producing a very exact portrait of the savage warrior.

Norman, who had been attending to his duties in the store, now returned, and looking over Sybil's shoulder exclaimed—

"Capital! It's Mysticoose himself." Snatching it from her hand, he held it up to the chief, saying, "What do you think of that, my friend? It's wonderfully like you, isn't it?"

Mysticoose started as he saw it, without making any reply; and rapidly advancing towards the young lady, endeavoured to take her hand. She instinctively drew back, and stepped behind Effie.

On meeting with this rebuff, the chief stopped short, and addressed Sybil, expressing in glowing language his admiration of her charms. Though she could not understand his words, she could not fail to suspect their meaning. Norman, however, who was sufficiently acquainted with the language of the Blackfeet to make out the meaning of the speech—though the expressions were too elaborate for him to follow —not possessing the discretion of his father, burst out laughing.

"What's all that you're saying?" he exclaimed. "Just face-about, and march out of this fort in double-quick time, or we may be obliged to send you off in a way you may not be pleased with."

Scarcely had Norman uttered these words, than the chief, placing his hand on the hilt of his scalping-knife, cast a glance full of anger at the speaker, but had so far command of himself as not to draw it.

Captain Mackintosh now saw that it was time to interfere, and, speaking in Indian, rebuked Norman for uncourteously treating their guest: and then, placing his hand in a friendly way on the shoulder of the chief, told him that he would consider the matter, advising him to retire, as it would be soon time for closing the gates of the fort, and expressing his regret that he could not, under the circumstances, afford him the hospitality he would have desired.

The chief appeared to be pacified, his countenance assuming its usual calm expression; and after he had cast another look of admiration at Sybil, he walked with a dignified step towards the gate.

Captain Mackintosh, who accompanied him, shook hands in a cordial way, and expressed a hope that nothing which had been said would cause a feeling of irritation to remain on his mind, and that he would continue to trade at the fort on the same friendly terms as hitherto. The chief made no reply, but stalked on towards his tents, which were pitched at some little distance from the fort. As soon as he had reached them, the gate was shut, and the usual guard placed to watch the proceedings of the Indians outside. The young ladies, who had agreed to take a ride with Norman, were somewhat disappointed on finding that Captain Mackintosh considered it would be imprudent for them to go outside the fort while Sybil's admirer remained in the neighbourhood.

"He is really a handsome fellow," said Norman, laughing, as he looked on the portrait. "You've done him justice too. Perhaps some day you may change your mind; though I cannot say that I should approve of his carrying you off to become Queen of the Roaring Bulls."

"Don't talk such nonsense, Norman," said Sybil. "I am vexed with myself for having gone out to take his portrait. I had no idea that the savage would even have looked at me. I have a great mind to tear up the picture."

"Pray don't do that," said Effie; "it is too well drawn to be destroyed, and I want to show it to mamma, who will, I am sure, admire it."

Mrs Mackintosh, who had been somewhat unwell, had not left her chamber; but in the evening she came into the sitting-room, when the portrait was shown her; and Norman related in his own way what had happened.

"I am sorry for it," she remarked. "I do not trust the Indians, and I am afraid that this savage chief may cause us some annoyance. I wish that you had not vexed him, Norman. You must in future be more cautious, and pray do not, on any account, go to a distance from the fort for some time to come. Sybil and Effie must give up their rides for the present, unless they go out with a strong party."

"My father doesn't think the fellow will trouble us, as we parted on good terms with him," answered Norman. "The chances are that he takes himself off to-morrow, and will speedily forget all about Sybil."

When Captain Mackintosh afterwards came in, though he tried to make light of the matter, his wife fancied that he looked much more anxious than usual.

Still Norman insisted that Mysticoose and his people would take their departure the next morning, and that they should then no longer be troubled by them.

Strict watch was kept at night, and all remained quiet in the Indian camp. Next morning the tents were still there, and no sign was perceived that the occupants had any intention of moving.

The day went by; but though the tents remained, the young chief did not make his appearance.

Norman was considerably put out. "I have no notion that the girls should be kept prisoners on account of an impudent Redskin," he exclaimed. "I will go out to the tents, and advise the chief and his party, now that they have transacted their business, to take themselves off."

"No, no, Norman, stay quiet, my lad," answered his father; "they'll not go faster for being ordered off; and it is just possible that the young chief may take it into his head to do you some harm. It will be a poor satisfaction to punish him afterwards."

"I am not afraid of him, or of any other savage like him," said Norman.

"Well, well, stay within the fort until I give you leave to go out," said his father. "Young blood quickly gets up, and a quarrel may ensue, which it is better to avoid."

Norman promised to obey; and, to vent his feelings by himself, went up to the platform, which was dignified by being called the ramparts, that he might take a look out, and ascertain if there were any signs of moving in the camp of the Blackfeet. He watched in vain, though he made out in the far distance two figures on the prairie going in a south-westerly direction. The sun was nearly setting when he returned to the house. He found his mother and Sybil engaged in their usual work.

"It is too provoking to have that fellow stopping out there, as if he were laying siege to the fort. My father won't allow me to go out, but I must get some one to inquire the chief's intentions. It is absurd in him to suppose that Sybil would ever be induced to marry him. He can have no object in remaining, as his admiration cannot be very deep, for he has only seen her once for a few minutes."

"I am not quite certain about that," remarked Sybil; "I think that he has seen me more than once. Don't you remember, when we were out riding, meeting with an Indian, whom you said was one of the Blackfeet, and who made Effie and me a long speech, though as we did not understand a word he said, we could not reply, but you talked to him, and laughed in his face. I thought that I recognised his features, though he was dressed and painted in so different a way that I may have been mistaken."

"I remember perfectly, but it never struck me that he was Mysticoose, though I cannot positively say that he was not," answered Norman. "I don't exactly remember what he said, but I fancy that he was praising the pale-faces generally, and expressing his desire to be their friend."

"Well, we cannot account for the wayward fancies of the Red men," observed Mrs Mackintosh; "but your father is anxious to retain their friendship, and would be unwilling to do anything to offend them. You must have patience; and I dare say in a day or two we shall be rid of our visitors."

"I am very sorry to have been the cause of the annoyance; and had I dreamed of the result, I would have kept out of the way of the chief," said Sybil, half laughing.

"Well, if the Blackfeet don't go to-morrow, something must be done to make them move off," exclaimed Hector.

Captain Mackintosh, though he did not say so, was really as much annoyed as his son.

No buffalo were to be seen in the neighbourhood, and it was evident, therefore, that the Indians did not remain for the sake of hunting. Among the men in the fort was an experienced *voyageur* and trapper, Le Brun by name, well versed in all Indian ways.

The captain having consulted him, he volunteered to go out

at night, and try to ascertain what the Indians were about.

"We must never trust those Redskins," he observed; "they don't remain here without an object."

His offer was accepted. Soon after dark he lowered himself down at the rear of the fort, and crept round, making a wide circuit, so that, should any of the Blackfeet be on the watch, he might escape observation. Captain Mackintosh directed a man to wait with a rope, to help him in again on the same side.

A careful look-out was kept during his absence round the fort. Some time having passed, and Le Brun not making his appearance, Captain Mackintosh began to fear that he had been discovered by the Indians, and captured. They would scarcely, however, he thought, venture to put him to death. Two hours or more went by; still he did not return. The Captain, therefore, began to consider whether it would be expedient to send out another man to try and ascertain what had happened. He was turning over in his mind who he should employ in this somewhat dangerous service, when Norman came up to him.

"Let me go," he said; "I am sure that I can get up to the camp without being discovered, and I will be exceedingly cautious. It is not, indeed, likely that the Indians will be on the watch; for, should they have caught Le Brun, they will not suppose that we shall send another person to look for him. I will only get near enough to hear what they are saying, and creep away again as noiselessly as a lynx."

"No, no, Norman; I am convinced of your courage and discretion, but I cannot allow you to risk your life for such an object," said his father.

"But I run no risk of losing my life," answered Norman; "they would not venture to kill me."

"They would not if they knew who you were; but finding a spy in their neighbourhood, they might shoot you down without inquiry," observed Captain Mackintosh.

"I don't want to be shot," said Norman; "depend upon it, I'll take good care to avoid that."

At length, Captain Mackintosh, reflecting that he could not send any one else on an expedition to the dangers of which he was unwilling to expose his own son, gave permission, charging Norman to approach the camp with the greatest possible caution, and only to do so provided he could hear the voices of the Indians, and had reason to believe that they were sitting in council.

Norman, well pleased at the confidence placed in him, hurried off to prepare for his expedition, by putting on a dark suit, which would assist in concealing him from view. Taking his gun, and sticking a brace of pistols in his belt, he descended, as Le Brun had done; but, to reach the camp, he took a route on the side opposite that which the scout had chosen. At first he walked upright, that he might the better ascertain the course to take. There were lights in each of the towers of the fort, which assisted him. No other objects were visible, even at the distance of a hundred yards. As he got nearer the tents, he hoped to be able to make them out against the sky. After he had gone some distance, he stooped down and began to creep along in the Indian fashion, trailing his gun. Every now and then he stopped to listen for sounds. He was, he calculated, approaching the camp, when he fancied he heard a rustling near him. It approached. He lay perfectly quiet. It might be a snake or some animal. His eyes were of but little assistance. "Should it be an Indian, I must try to take the fellow prisoner; but it may be a hard matter to do that, unless he is unarmed, and then I must hold a pistol to his head, and threaten to shoot him if he cries out."

He had scarcely thought this, when he saw the head of a man lifted up as if going to gaze around. Strong and active, with good nerves, he was about to spring on the person, and seize him by the throat, when the other must have made him out, and he heard a voice whisper—

"C'est moi, Le Brun!"

Norman, greatly relieved, made himself known.

"Venez avec moi, vite!" and the Canadian led the way, crawling along the ground towards the lights glimmering from the fort. It was not until they had been hauled up, and were safe inside, that Le Brun spoke. He had, he told Captain Mackintosh, got close up to the camp, where he heard the sounds of many voices, and the tramp of feet, as if a large number of persons were collected, although only one fire burned in the midst of the tents. He was afraid of approaching nearer, lest he should be discovered. He waited in the expectation that the leaders would gather round the fire, as is their wont, to discuss their plans. He was rewarded for his patience, although they were too far off to enable him to see them distinctly. He, however, counted at least six warriors, who took their places at the fire, and one after the other got up and addressed their companions. A few words only reached him; but he heard enough to be convinced that they were discussing a plan to take possession of the fort, but its details he was unable to make out. He had gone round the camp, and while returning on the side opposite to that from which he had set off, had fallen in with Norman.

"We must take care to be doubly vigilant, then," said Captain Mackintosh.

He at once cautioned the men to be on the watch; but before the ladies he made light of the matter, not wishing to cause them unnecessary anxiety. He felt pretty certain, indeed, that the Blackfeet would not openly attempt to take the fort, even though their numbers had, as Le Brun supposed, been much increased.

Night passed away without the slightest alarm. The next day matters remained to all appearance as on the preceding one. The tents were there, and a few Indians only—some on horseback, others on foot—were seen moving about in the neighbourhood, but none came near the fort. Le Brun suggested that if they had any treacherous design in view, they were probably waiting until the hunters, who made excursions to bring in game two or three times a week, had been seen to leave the fort, and that they would then, when fewer people were within, try and carry out their plan, whatever that might be. He suggested that a party should leave the fort after mid-day with several pack horses, as if they intended to make a long excursion. That they should go away to the south-east, and, as soon as they were out of sight, cross the river and come back again after dark, on the north side. If the Indians really intended treachery, they would certainly take the opportunity of attempting to carry it out.

Captain Mackintosh approved of the plan, and Norman thought it an excellent one. "I should so like to disappoint those rascals, and catch them in their own trap," he said.

The horses (or the guard, as the stud belonging to a fort is called) were kept in a meadow on the opposite side of the river, where they were tolerably safe from any attempts which the marauding bands on the south might make to carry them off. Some time passed before those required could be brought across. As soon as they arrived, Le Brun, with eight well-armed men, with as many spare horses, set off on their pretended hunting expedition. They took care to pass sufficiently near the Indian camp to be easily seen.

"Le Brun was right in his suspicions!" exclaimed Norman from the ramparts, addressing his father, who was walking below. "Here comes Mysticoose with a dozen followers, dressed in their gayest attire, for I can see their ornaments glistening in the rays of the sun. Perhaps he has come to ask for Sybil's answer to his offer; if so, we can give him a very short one."

"We will say nothing to offend him," answered Captain Mackintosh, who had joined his son; "but it will be prudent, knowing what we do, not to admit these gentlemen inside the gate. I will go out and meet them, and you and the other men cover me with your rifles. Let the Indians have a glimpse of your arms, and I am sure that they will attempt no violence.' The arrangements were quickly made. As soon as the chief and his party drew near, Captain Mackintosh went out of the fort, directing the men at the gate to close it should the Indians show any intention of making a rush to get in.

Advancing a short distance, he called to Mysticoose to dismount, and explain the object of his visit. The chief looked up at the ramparts, and, seeing the gleaming rifle-barrels, did as he was directed. Giving the bridle of his horse to one of his followers, he then advanced, and, putting out his hand in a cordial manner, said—

"Why does my white brother look upon me as an enemy? I have traded fairly, and wish to trade again. I have now brought some more peltries, not to trade, but to present to him as an earnest of my goodwill. Let him, then, admit me and my followers within the gates, that I may offer my present as presents should be offered, and have the happiness of gazing once more on the fair lily of the prairie, after whom my heart pants, as does the weary stag for the refreshing stream." Mysticoose uttered much more in the same strain before he stopped.

Captain Mackintosh replied that he was always glad to see his friend, but as it was late in the day he regretted that he could not admit the chief and his followers, but that the next morning, if they wished to come, he should be happy to receive them; and although he would not refuse the present they had brought, he must insist on returning one of equal value in goods, as he could not promise that the fair lily, as he described his daughter, would be willing to show herself, and begged the chief to understand clearly that she had sufficiently considered the matter, and could not become his bride.

Whatever were the Indian's feelings, he concealed them, and made an equally courteous reply, intimating that, notwithstanding what his white brother had said, he should come as proposed with a larger present, and a greater number of followers to convey it. He then, shaking hands as before, returned to his horse, and remounting, rode off with his companions.

"I hope, after all, that the Indian intends no treachery," observed Captain Mackintosh, as he re-entered the fort; and the gates were closed for the night. "Still we must be on our guard."

"I should think so, sir," said Norman; "and we shall soon hear what Le Brun has to say on the subject."

About a couple of hours after dark, Le Brun and his party arrived, and, having left their horses on the other side of the stream, noiselessly entered the fort.

At an early hour the next day the young chief, with nearly twenty followers, was seen approaching. Captain Mackintosh at once placed his men in positions commanding the entrance, so that, should the Indians show any treacherous intentions, the gate might forthwith be shut. His great object was to prevent bloodshed; at the same time, while showing that he was not unprepared for treachery, he did not wish to offend his guest.

As a precautionary measure, he resolved not to admit more than half their number, and he placed men ready to close the gates directly the party had entered. Mysticoose rode up with the air of a gallant in days of yore, and throwing the rein to one of his attendants, he, with the larger number of his followers, dismounted and advanced towards Captain Mackintosh, who stood ready to receive him.

"I can only allow ten to enter," said the captain; "the rest must remain outside with the horses."

The chief, appearing not to think this unreasonable, directed the rest of his followers to keep back. His countenance fell, however, when, having entered the gate, he looked round and saw the hunters whom he supposed to be at a distance, standing on either side with arms in their hands. He hesitated and stopped short.

"Does my white brother think I come intending treachery?" he asked. "He has been deceived by some one. My object is to present these peltries to him, hoping that he will give me, not the goods he spoke of, but the fair lily, his daughter, and I will promise to bring him ten times the amount before another summer has begun."

Captain Mackintosh replied that he had already said all that he could say on that subject.

But the chief was not satisfied with his refusal, and began another long speech, which, as Norman remarked, "Though it might have a head, there seemed but little chance of seeing its tail." He advised his father to try and cut it short.

Meantime, Le Brun, having slipped away, unseen by the Indians, had gone up on the ramparts, crept round to a part whence he could observe their tents. He had not been long there when he saw a large body of men issuing forth, and rapidly approaching the fort. Hurrying down, he gave the information to Captain Mackintosh.

"There is no time to lose, monsieur," he said. "If we don't turn these fellows out, they'll try to obtain possession of the fort, as I suspect they all along intended to do."

On hearing this, Captain Mackintosh ordered his men, who had been drawn up on either side, to close round their visitors, and some, who had been concealed, to show themselves.

The chief, on seeing this, stopped short in his speech, knowing that his treacherous design, it such he had intended, must have been discovered.

"What does this mean?" he asked, in a tone which showed that his self-confident air was more assumed than real.

"It means, my friend, that you must quit the fort if you do not wish to be shut up within it, and come another day to finish your address," answered Captain Mackintosh. "I wish to be your friend, but I must be obeyed."

The appearance of the garrison showed the chief that the captain was in earnest; and though he and his followers looked as if they were about to make a rush, thinking better of it, they beat a hasty retreat, when the gate was closed behind them. This was not done too soon, for they had got but a short distance off when a number of warriors from the camp, uttering loud shouts, galloped up, evidently expecting to indulge in the plunder of the fort. The young chief, no longer able to constrain the rage he felt at his disappointment, turning round, made gestures significant of his intended vengeance; then, putting spurs to his horse, he galloped off beyond range of any rifle-shot which he might well have expected would be sent after him. He was seen at a distance haranguing his people; but if he was urging them at once to attack the fort, they did not appear willing to risk their lives in an attempt which was likely to prove a failure.

The following day, having struck camp, they moved away to the southward, and Le Brun, who followed them to a considerable distance, reported that they appeared to have no intention of stopping in the neighbourhood, but were probably returning to the lodges of their tribe.

Greatly relieved by this information, the inmates of Fort Duncan pursued their usual avocations without any apprehension of further annoyance from Mysticoose and his people.

CHAPTER FOUR

We must now return to the two travellers and their strange guide. Although Loraine had slept but little the previous night, he could not close his eyes. He enjoyed the excitement of the life he was leading, but he did not hide from himself its dangers, and he felt the responsibility of having induced young Hector to accompany him. He was also anxious to arrive at the fort, for he had become much interested in its inmates. Although it was supposed that the Blackfeet had gone to the westward, he thought it possible that some of them might have remained behind, and followed up the trail of his party. He had, however, great confidence in the watchfulness of Greensnake, and he hoped also that the dogs would give due notice should any enemies approach.

"If we pass over this night in safety, I think that we shall get through the rest of our journey without difficulty," he said to himself. "We have accomplished well-nigh fifty miles to-day, and, as our horses will have a good feed to-night, we may ride another fifty to-morrow, and by keeping that up, we shall, as far as I can calculate, reach Fort Duncan in four or five days."

He was about to drop off to sleep, when he was again aroused by a continuous howl in the distance. After listening for some time, he was convinced that it was produced by

W. H. G. Kingston

wolves. He fancied from the sound that there must have been hundreds of them. It grew nearer and nearer. The animals were coming that way. They might attack him and Hector, or, at all events, the horses, and either kill them or put them to flight.

He looked at the fire. By their guide's advice he had allowed it to burn low, so that no flames casting their light around should betray the position of the camp to prowling Indians. Still it was better, he thought, to run even that risk than to allow the savage brutes to get into the camp. He, therefore, having thrown some more sticks on the fire, which quickly blazed up, awoke Hector, who naturally inquired what was the matter.

"Do you not hear the howling of wolves?" asked Loraine. "Get your rifle ready."

"But Greensnake advised us not to fire, lest we should discover our camp to the Indians," said Hector; "and I don't fancy that at this time of the year wolves would be daring enough to attack us."

"They may, however, attack the horses," answered Loraine. "I will go and warn him, so that he may collect them."

"He is on the alert, depend upon that," said Hector; "and well knows what to do."

"It is wise to be on the safe side," answered Loraine, getting up. "Stay by our saddles and provisions, and I will try to find him." He set off towards where he supposed the horses were feeding.

As soon as he had got beyond the range of the light thrown from the fire, the darkness became so great that he could with difficulty avoid running against the trunks of the trees. He stretched out his gun before him to try and feel the way. Two or three times he saved himself by this precaution. At last he thought that he must have reached the spot where Greensnake ought to be found; but though he called out to him, no answer came. He shouted louder and louder, still there was no reply, nor could he distinguish the forms of any of the horses against the sky. He could hear, however, the sound of the yelping and barking of the wolves, apparently much nearer than before. Still he went on, forgetting that he ran the risk of losing sight of the fire. At length, turning round to look for it, intending to go back to the camp, what was his dismay on being unable to discover the slightest glimmering of light in any direction! He had proceeded further than he had supposed, and regretted his folly, for he was well aware how easily he might lose himself. The sky overhead was obscured, so that the stars afforded him no guide. He thought that he had turned completely round, but of this he could not be quite certain, and he feared that by going on he might only get further and further from the fire. He shouted out—

"Hector, Hector, don't move; but only shout in return, that I may know where to find you."

Instead of Hector's voice, the barking and yelping of the wolves alone reached his ear. Probably his shouts had been drowned by the fearful din they had been making. They served, however, partly to guide him; but they seemed so near that he expected every moment to be assailed by them; and in the darkness it would be a difficult matter to defend himself. Still, being a man of courage and determination, he resolved to face the danger; and keeping as direct a course as the impediments in his way would allow, he directed his steps towards the spot whence it appeared to him the sounds proceeded. He, of course, could move but slowly. He had

W. H. G. Kingston

gone, as he supposed, far enough to reach the camp, or, at all events, to be in sight of the fire, when he heard a shot, which came, it seemed to him, from a point rather more to the left than that towards which he was making his way. He had no doubt that it had been fired by Hector, and he immediately turned, hoping soon to catch sight of the fire. He was unwilling to discharge his own gun, not knowing at what moment he might require it to defend himself from the wolves. He, therefore, only shouted as before. He listened, and fancied that above the yelping chorus he could distinguish Hector's voice. Presently, to his infinite relief, he caught sight of the gleam of the fire, more distant, however, than he had supposed it could possibly be. He made towards it as fast as he could venture to move; notwithstanding his caution, he first ran against a tree, and soon afterwards stumbled at a fallen log.

He could now clearly distinguish the spot where the fire was burning, by the lurid light which it cast on the neighbouring trees; and, with more confidence than before, he was hurrying on, when he saw to his right a number of glowing eyeballs, and the yelping of the wolves sounded closer than ever.

Waiting until a pair of the glowing balls were only a few feet off, he fired. They disappeared. A fearful yell from the whole pack followed. He could see a number of dark forms surrounding him. There was no time to reload, so, clubbing his rifle, he swept it round and round on every side. He felt it striking every now and then on the heads of the creatures which were thus providentially kept at bay. The fire became more distinct; but the wolves continued to leap and snarl and yelp as savagely as at first; and, notwithstanding the blows he was dealing about, one of the brutes seized him by the coat, and another, still more daring, flew at his throat, and though it failed to bite him, caught him by the collar, and it was with the greatest difficulty that he saved himself from being dragged down. He was afraid that Hector, hearing the sound of the wolves, and not seeing him, might fire; he, therefore, shouted at the top of his voice, to show his whereabouts. Presently, he saw his young friend holding a couple of flaming brands in his hands, come rushing towards him, accompanied by the two dogs, who, springing forward with furious barks, attacked his savage assailants. The assistance came only just in time, for the wolves had nearly succeeded in pulling him to the ground. The dogs at once sprang upon the brute hanging to his collar, which let go its hold to defend itself, when a blow on its head from Loraine's rifle prevented it from offering further resistance. The dogs then flew at the other wolf, which also let go; while Hector, dashing the burning brands in the faces of the rest of the pack, put them to flight, enabling him and Loraine to get back almost breathless to the camp. The brave dogs were following the wolves, and would probably soon have been torn to pieces had they not promptly been called back.

"What can have become of Greensnake?" exclaimed Hector, as soon as they had time and breath to speak. "I hope that he has not played us false, and gone off with the horses."

"I have no fear of that," answered Loraine. "The old hunter would not have sent him with us unless he had perfect confidence in his honesty. Perhaps he heard the wolves coming long before we did, and took them to some place of security."

"He was more likely to have driven them into the camp, where we could have assisted in protecting them," observed Hector. "I am afraid that he has been surprised by a band of Blackfeet, or Sircees, who are notorious horse-stealers, and that they have carried off him as well as the animals. If so, we shall be left in a pretty plight."

"We have our guns and dogs, and a fair stock of ammunition, to obtain food, and our compass to guide us; and if we find that we have lost our horses, we must push forward on foot," answered Loraine. "But I am grievously annoyed at the prospect of being unable to reach the fort as soon as we expected; however, we must try to make our way on foot, and although we may be longer about it than we had hoped, we may still arrive in time to be of service. It is useless, however, talking over the matter at present. The best thing you can do is to lie down, and get some sleep while I keep watch."

"No, no," said Hector. "I have had my share already; but pray do you lie down, and I will watch."

At length Loraine consented to do this, expecting to be able to arouse himself in a short time; while Hector, taking his rifle in hand, began to walk up and down, anxiously looking out for Greensnake. The wolves, however, still snarling and yelping a short distance off, would, it at length occurred to him, prevent the guide from making his appearance till the morning. Having now time for thought, he recollected the warning Greensnake had given; and he reflected that possibly at any moment, should a party of Blackfeet have been in the neighbourhood, and heard the reports of their rifles, guided by the light of their fire, they might come suddenly upon them. He kept, therefore, a vigilant watch with his ears rather than his eyes, listening for any sound which might indicate their approach, and trusting also to the dogs, which were on the alert, and accompanied him whenever he moved a few feet from the camp. When he returned they went back again, and lay down near the fire, with their noses on their paws, and ears erect, showing that they were wide awake.

At length Loraine awoke, and insisted on Hector's lying

down, who, before he did so, mentioned the ideas which had occurred to him.

"Never mind now what you think, but go to sleep," said Loraine. "I'll keep a bright look-out; depend upon that."

Soon after this the wolves, attracted possibly by a passing stag or some other game, greatly to his relief, scampered off, their cries becoming less and less distinct as they got to a distance.

The night seemed interminably long, but the morning came at length. Loraine aroused Hector, and having made up the fire, intending to come back for breakfast, he charged the dogs to watch over the baggage, and then set out in search of Greensnake and the horses. Loraine endeavoured to trace the course he had taken during the night, but the trail was so indistinct that he could not be certain in what direction he had gone. As he and Hector advanced, they looked round for the horses, but they were not near the spot to which Greensnake had taken them on the previous evening, nor were they anywhere to be seen. They came, however, upon what Hector believed were their tracks; but as they were scattered about over a wide space of ground, he could not be positive as to what course they had taken. Loraine still argued that the guide would return, and that it would be prudent to go back to camp and wait for his appearance. This they accordingly did, shooting on their way a couple of ducks, which served them for breakfast, the remains being given to the dogs. After some time Loraine went to the top of the highest point near at hand—a small knoll or hillock—that he might take a look-out for the missing horses, but he soon came back without having seen them.

"I think we should wait a little longer," he observed. "The young Indian may have thought it prudent to go to a considerable distance on account of the wolves. He may have slept until the morning, or may have stopped to catch and cook some food."

"I will have another look round," said Hector. "A few ducks won't come amiss, if I can kill them on the way, either to us or our dogs, before we finally make a start;" and, calling the two dogs, he set off, they willingly accompanying him.

While Hector was away from the camp Loraine thoughtfully employed himself in examining their baggage, and in selecting such articles of food and clothing as they could carry on their backs, and in doing them up in two packs, making the heaviest for himself. He was thus engaged when he heard a couple of shots, but concluding that Hector had fired at some ducks, as he proposed, went on with his occupation. As he looked at their saddle-bags and valises, he regretted having to leave them, but without horses he saw no possibility of carrying them. Noon was approaching, Hector had not returned, and he became seriously anxious; so, taking his gun, he set out to look for him. "If he returns while I am away, he will, I hope, guess why I have gone, and will remain quietly here for my return," he said to himself. As he walked along he searched on every side, but Hector was nowhere to be seen. The dreadful thought occurred that his young friend might have met with some accident, or that, should Indians have carried off Greensnake, they might have entrapped him also. His own position was trying in the extreme; but being a man of courage, he nerved himself up to encounter whatever might happen. As he was casting his eyes around, he caught sight of a small, dark object on the ground. He hastened on. It was a powder-flask. It, however, was certainly not Hector's. He had no doubt that it belonged to Greensnake. A short distance beyond he came on a ramrod. The ground was covered with a rich grass, and there were signs of horses having fed on it, so that no doubt remained on his mind that it was here Greensnake had been during the night, and on further examination he discovered traces of the animals' feet moving to the eastward, but he was unable to ascertain whether Hector had passed that way. Had he done so, he would probably have followed up the trail of the horses. Loraine, therefore, hurried on in the same direction. He marked as carefully as he could the course he was taking, examining his compass to guide himself. Several times he thought that it would be better to retrace his steps, lest Hector should have returned during his absence to the camp. He was at length on the point of doing so when he saw before him a wood. At the same instant, he fancied that he heard the bark of a dog. He hurried forward, feeling sure that it was that either of Muskey or Buster, and he hoped that, if so, Hector was not far off, and had escaped being captured by Indians. In a short time he again heard the dogs bark, and as he approached the wood a voice, which he knew was Hector's, shouted out—

"Take care, there's a big she-grizzly, with a couple of cubs, in that thicket. I wounded her, and she's very savage."

"Where are you?" asked Loraine.

"Here, up a tree," cried Hector. "Whenever I attempt to descend, she rushes out, and I have dropped my gun, so that I have no chance of killing her."

"Come down then, and find your gun, and I will stand by to shoot the bear if she appears."

"She got hold of my gun and broke it to pieces, so that you must not depend upon my help," cried Hector. "You'll do better to get up here, and kill her when she shows herself."

"I'll take post behind the tree, and when she sees you

descending, perhaps she will come out from the cover," answered Loraine. The dogs meantime were barking furiously outside the thicket.

No sooner did Hector begin to descend than the bear, which had apparently had her eyes fixed on him, came waddling out from her place of concealment, growling savagely. The two dogs wisely scampered off out of her reach, and Hector sprang up again. Loraine then stepped out from behind the trunk, when the bear rose on her hind quarters, growling and showing her fangs. The opportunity was as favourable as he could desire. He took a steady aim, and over she rolled. At this, Hector gave a shout of satisfaction, while the dogs came back, though afraid to approach, as she was still struggling violently. Loraine then reloaded, and advancing, sent another shot crashing through her brain. The two cubs had come out, and looked as if inclined to give battle, but the dogs kept them at bay, giving time to Loraine to load again, when he fired and killed one of them, and the next was settled in the same way.

Hector, who had come down from his perch, expressed his regret at having caused his friend so much anxiety. He had been following up the track of the horses, when he caught sight of the bear, which he unwisely fired at and wounded. She at first had gone off with her cubs, but just as he had reached the wood, she had turned and rushed at him. He had again fired, but having no time to reload, in attempting to escape up the tree had dropped his gun, when the bear, seizing it, had gnawed and twisted it in such a manner as to render it perfectly useless. Had not the dogs held her in check, he acknowledged that he should have been caught.

"Had we our horses, we might supply ourselves with bears' flesh sufficient to last for the whole of our journey; as it is, we can only take as much as we can conveniently carry,' observed Loraine. They speedily, if not very scientifically, cut off a portion of the meat, which they did up with strips of the cubs' hides into two packages, the dogs meantime enjoying a magnificent feast off the remains. They then retired to the camp, still as much in the dark as ever as to what had become of Greensnake and the horses.

"I don't know what I shall do without my gun," said Hector, as they walked along. "If we meet with enemies, I shall be unable to help you to fight; nor can I kill any game."

Loraine did his best to comfort him. "We must keep out of the way of enemies, and my gun will enable me to obtain as much food as we shall require, while you can assist me with your advice, as you know more about the country than I do," he observed.

When Loraine pointed to the articles they must abandon, Hector suggested that they should be placed *en cache* by hanging them up to the bough of a tree, deep in the wood, so as to be concealed from passers-by.

They might thus some day have an opportunity of sending for them.

"There, you see how at once you can help me," remarked Loraine. "I have been sadly puzzled to know what to do with them."

Having taken a substantial meal of bears' flesh, they carefully put out their fire, and obliterated as far as they could the traces of their encampment. They then strapped on their packs, and Hector supplying himself with a pointed stick, in the place of his damaged rifle, they set off, followed by the dogs, in the direction, as they supposed, of Fort Duncan.

CHAPTER FIVE

For many a mile the weary travellers tramped on. In vain they looked out for Greensnake, and had too much reason to fear that he had been entrapped by the Blackfeet, and probably murdered. The country, though often fertile and beautiful, was in some places sandy and barren, and utterly destitute of water. The whole day, their flasks having been emptied, they had not a drop to quench their burning thirst, and when they did at length reach a pool, the liquid in it was so bitter and stagnant that they dared scarcely to taste a drop, even after straining it through a handkerchief. The food they had brought with them was also running short, and they had been unable to shoot any game to supply its place. Two or three buffalo had been seen in the distance, but had made off before they could get within shot; and several deer had passed, but being to leeward, scented them, and scampered away as they approached.

"Though we cannot find large game, we must look out for small," observed Hector. "Perhaps we shall meet with some beavers, musk-rats, or badgers; we must not be particular."

"Not if we are starving," answered Loraine; "but I should prefer a hare or duck, or a prairie-hen."

At length a broad stream appeared before them. They hurried

forward to quench their thirst, and then sat down to consider how it was to be crossed. They could both swim, but their packs and Loraine's gun, as well as their clothes, had to be floated across.

There are, fortunately, neither alligators nor voracious fish in the rivers of those latitudes, and so Hector proposed that they should build a raft of rushes and dried branches on which to place their clothes, their packs, and the gun, and tow it over.

It was soon formed, though Loraine feared it was a some-what frail structure, even for the duty it was intended to perform.

The passage was accomplished with difficulty, and with the loss of Loraine's gun, which slipped off into the deepest water.

They lamented this serious loss, but Loraine having supplied himself with a pointed stick, they set off, endeavouring to keep up each other's spirits as they marched on. They had still their compass to steer by, but their direct progress was on some days very slow, as they had to turn aside to avoid extensive marshes and lakelets. Their food at length came to an end, and, in spite of all Hector's efforts, he was unable to trap any animals. They several times saw beavers, which got away from them, and the ducks and other water-fowls only appeared to fly off with derisive quacks at their impotent attempts to knock them down, so Hector declared.

The dogs were growing thinner and thinner, and at length Buster, who had dropped behind, did not come up to them. In vain they called him, but, unwilling to lose time by returning, they went on, hoping that the dog would overtake them at their camp. He did not appear, however.

"Perhaps he took it into his head that we might eat him," said Hector, looking at poor Muskey, who wagged his tail as he spoke, wondering if he was to have anything for supper.

"Should you mind eating Muskey?" asked Hector.

"I should be very unwilling to kill the poor dog; but if we can find no food to-morrow, it must be done, I fear, to save our lives," answered Loraine.

Although they lighted a fire, they lay down that night supperless. At daybreak they set off, hoping to reach a lakelet in which Hector thought that he might catch some white fish. They were becoming faint, and no water was to be seen. At length they entered a wood, close to which they found an abundance of choke-berries, as well as gooseberries and currants, which served to appease the gnawings of hunger, although the poor dog looked as if he wished that he could have something more substantial; and about mid-day, they each managed, almost at the same moment, to knock over a small bird.

So great was their hunger that they immediately halted, and, lighting a fire, cooked and ate them.

Darkness coming on, all hope of obtaining food that night was given up. Loraine offered to kill Muskey.

"No, no; let him live to-night, and perhaps to-morrow morning he may assist in catching something," answered Hector.

They lay down close to the fire, but neither could for some time sleep. Hector was very feverish, and Loraine himself began to feel ill. He saw that his young companion was very unlikely to be able to proceed, and he determined to set off next morning in search of water. At last he closed his eyes, and, to his surprise, when he awoke he found that the sun had arisen. Hector was still sleeping. The fire had gone out, and Muskey lay with his nose on his paws, watching his masters.

"I must manage to get the dog to remain behind and guard him," he thought; "I will try to find water by myself."

Hector awoke just as he was about to set off, and tried to get up; but his strength failed, and he sank down again on the ground.

"Hold out for a few hours longer, and I trust I shall obtain relief for you," said Loraine. "Get Muskey to stay, and he will assist in defending you should any enemies appear."

To prevent the dog from following him, Loraine fastened a strap round its neck, and put the end into Hector's hand. The dog, making no resistance, lay down by his side. Loraine set off towards a knoll which he saw at a little distance, hoping from thence to be able to ascertain in what direction water was to be found. He walked as fast as his strength would allow. On reaching the knoll he looked anxiously round on every side. Before long he saw what appeared to be the gleam of water, near a wood of willow and aspen, and tottered forward, every instant expecting to find the water, but it seemed to be further off than he had supposed. At last he saw the grove of willows, and he was sure that the water would be found near it. The grove was reached, but no water could he see. "It must be close at hand," he said aloud; "it would be useless to attempt returning until I have found it." By a strenuous effort he aroused himself, and pushed forward. His strength was failing: he felt as if he were in a dream. In vain he tried to move his feet. At length he sank fainting to the ground, beneath the shade of a tree.

W. H. G. Kingston

How long he had thus remained, he could not tell, when he heard a human voice. At first he thought it was Hector calling to him for help. He tried to rise, but before he could regain his feet he sank back to his former position.

"This is dreadful, ' he thought. "I must help that poor lad. His friends at the fort, if we do not reach it, will be surprised by savages and cut off. Those two young girls—what a dreadful fate will be theirs! I must try and recover myself." And once more he endeavoured to get up. Again he heard a voice; it was much nearer; and opening his eyes, he saw a figure standing over him. It was that of Isaac Sass.

"Right glad I am to find you!" exclaimed the old man, stooping down; "but you seem in a sad plight. What has become of your young companion? I trust no harm has befallen him."

"Water, water!" answered Loraine, faintly. "Take water to him; he wants it more than I do."

"You want it bad enough, I guess," said the trapper; and, unslinging his flask, he poured some of the refreshing liquid down Loraine's throat. It quickly revived him.

"Take him water," he said; "he is out there." And he pointed in the direction where he had left Hector.

The old man shouted; and, presently, who should appear but Greensnake, mounted on a horse, accompanied by three others, which he at once secured to some neighbouring trees. Isaac then handed a flask of water to the young Indian, who, receiving some directions which Loraine could not understand, set off at full gallop towards the spot where Hector had been left.

"Will he find him?" asked Loraine, anxiously.

"No fear of that," said Sass. "When you have recovered we will follow. Here, take some food, if you can swallow it."

Loraine was better able to eat than he expected.

"I brought a couple of horses for you and your companion, besides yonder pack animal; for I guessed whereabouts I should find you, though I thought you would have made better progress than you have done, and I did not expect to come upon your trail for another day or two."

Loraine having briefly explained what had happened, inquired how the old trapper had fallen in with Greensnake.

"The lad was carried off by a party of Sircees, who stole your horses; but, believing him to be an idiot, they failed to keep a watch over him, and he easily managed to escape on one of the fleetest of their animals, and made his way towards Fort Edmonton. I, knowing the difficulties you would be in without horses, at once set off to find you, though I little expected that you would have been reduced to this sad plight. And now do you think you could mount, and see how it fares with your friend?"

"I will try, at all events," said Loraine, feeling very anxious about Hector.

With the aid of the old trapper he got into the saddle. When once there he felt capable of going as fast as the horse could gallop.

They set off, the trapper leading the other horse. As they neared the spot, Loraine's mind misgave him. Had Hector survived the hardships he had endured? He himself felt how nearly he had succumbed, and he wished that he had begged the old trapper to go on at once, and left the Indian with him.

"Cheer up, cheer up, friend," said Sass, surmising the thoughts passing through his mind. "Youth is tough, and hunger and thirst don't kill a man for a long time."

At last the spot was reached. Loraine threw himself from his horse, and nearly fell to the ground in doing so, forgetting how weak he was. Greensnake was bending over Hector, supporting his head with one hand, while he was feeding him with the other; Musky, who was looking on, evidently having recognised the Indian as a friend.

Loraine hurried forward.

"All right," exclaimed Sass; "speak to your friend, my boy."

"Yes, yes, thanks to this Indian," answered Hector, faintly.

"I knew it would be so," observed old Sass, addressing Loraine. "We'll camp here, as neither of you are fit for travelling, and while you attend to the lad, Greensnake and I will light a fire and put up a hut for you, and then I'll see about getting some game."

These arrangements were soon made, and old Sass set off with his gun to shoot any creature he might come across fit for the pot.

Hector had so far recovered as to be able to sit up, and to show that he was likely to do justice to the fare the old trapper expected to provide for the party.

CHAPTER SIX

The inhabitants of Fort Duncan were spending their time much as usual, and had almost ceased to trouble themselves about the threats of Mysticoose, who had, they believed, returned to his lodges, having seen the hopelessness of inducing the English chief to give him his daughter in marriage. The hunters were out every day in search of buffalo, sometimes several days together, while the young ladies, accompanied by their father and brother, and two or three attendants, took their rides as they had been accustomed to do, without fear of encountering enemies.

They were about, one afternoon, to take a ride, when a small party of mounted Indians—who, as they had several pack horses, were evidently coming to trade—were seen approaching the fort.

"We must wait to receive these fellows," said Captain Mackintosh, "and I am afraid, my girls, there will be little chance for you afterwards to get your gallop."

"Oh, papa, Norman can come with us, if you can spare him; it would be a pity to lose this lovely day," said Effie.

Sybil said nothing, and Captain Mackintosh, perhaps against his better judgment, consented to let the girls go, supposing

W. H. G. Kingston

that the new comers would be too fully engaged in trading to notice them. They accordingly mounted, and accompanied by Norman and two of the men who usually acted as their body guard, set out a short time before the Indians arrived at the camp.

No one in the fort observed that one of the savages turned round his horse and galloped off in the direction from whence they had come.

As there were not more than a dozen men, and as they, according to custom, had deposited their arms outside the fort, they were admitted without hesitation.

Captain Mackintosh, well acquainted with the various Indian nations, was struck by the appearance of their features, which were those of the Blackfeet, although they wore none of the distinctive ornaments of that tribe, and introduced themselves as Peagons, whose territory lies to the southward. Their chief, a plausibly mannered man, stated that they had been induced to come to Fort Duncan by hearing that better value was given for peltries there than was to be obtained from the Long Knives. They seemed, however, in no hurry to begin business, and begged that food might be provided for the party, as they had gone several days without shooting a buffalo, hinting that some fire-water would be a welcome addition, though they did not appear surprised when Captain Mackintosh refused to supply the pernicious beverage.

The visitors did ample justice to the feast placed before them, and would apparently have continued eating as long as any meat remained, had not Captain Mackintosh suggested that darkness would come on before they had time to commence trading.

At length, therefore, one of the packs was undone, and

business proceeded in the usual way.

They were thus engaged, when a little hump-backed Indian, whom nobody had observed, crept in at the gate of the fort, and making his way up to where Captain Mackintosh was superintending affairs, drew a piece of paper from a leathern pouch and put it into his hand.

Captain Mackintosh having read it attentively, directing his head clerk to go on with the trading, beckoned to the hump-backed Indian to accompany him out of ear-shot of the trading party, and having questioned him and received his answers, he summoned Le Brun.

Though the Captain had betrayed no emotion in presence of the strange looking little Indian, his chief hunter remarked his agitation. "What has happened, Monsieur Capitaine?" he asked.

"This is a matter of life and death, and I know that I can trust you, Le Brun," said Captain Mackintosh, not directly answering him. "Take the fleetest of our horses and ride after Monsieur Norman and the young ladies. Spare neither spur nor whip. Desire them to return immediately to the fort, as hard as they can gallop. Here, take this with you," and he wrote a few words on a slip of paper to be delivered to Norman.

"Monsieur Capitaine can depend on me. I will make La Froule fly like the whirlwind," said Le Brun, and doubling up the paper, he hurried away to obey the order he had received.

"I would that I could go myself," murmured Captain Mackintosh, "but my duty compels me to be here, and even for my dear children's sake, I must not desert my post when

W. H. G. Kingston

danger threatens."

It was some time before Le Brun could catch the horse he had selected.

Captain Mackintosh endeavoured to conceal his anxiety, especially from his visitors, whose keen eyes had been watching him narrowly though in no other way did they show that they suspected the little hump-backed Indian had come with any information relating to them. Captain Mackintosh, who had gone up to the platform, gave a sigh of relief, as he at length saw Le Brun gallop off at full speed in the direction the riding party had taken.

Having seen Le Brun off, Captain Mackintosh returned to superintend the trading, which the Indians seemed inclined to prolong more than usual. They haggled over every article, and insisted on their peltries being weighed more than once, on the pretence that there was some mistake, or that the scales were out of order. They examined the goods offered to them over and over again, handing them round to each other, and criticising their quality. They then requested that tobacco might be supplied to them, as they were inclined to have a smoke before proceeding further.

One of them then got up and spoke. The meaning of his speech was difficult to understand, though uttered with that flow of language of which most Indians have the command.

Captain Mackintosh bore all this with the necessary patience He did not wish to come to a rupture with his visitors, though from the warning he had received, he strongly suspected that treachery was intended.

As time went on, he became more and more anxious at not seeing the girls and Hector return.

At length he went to the platform, but not a glimpse of the riding party could he discover. On his return he found the Indians still smoking their pipes. He inquired whether they intended to sell the remainder of their peltries, when one of them getting up stated that they wished to hold a council on the subject, and asked permission to sleep in the fort, that they might be prepared the next morning to continue their trading.

Captain Mackintosh replied that he had made it a rule to allow no strangers to sleep within the fort, that they might leave their peltries if they chose, that they would be perfectly safe, and that they could sleep in the hut built expressly for the purpose outside the gate.

This answer appeared somewhat to disconcert the traders, and one of them rising, offered to go on again with the business after they had been supplied with some more food, for which, as he expressed it, their souls yearned.

Captain Mackintosh answered that a feast should be prepared for them, but that as the gates were closed at a certain hour, they must not take it amiss at being requested to leave the fort before that time.

While their spokesman was making his address, the dark eyes of the other Indians were wandering around in every direction. Perhaps they began to have an idea that their intentions were suspected, when they perceived that all the men in the fort had pistols in their belts, and swords by their sides, and their rifles in their hands.

While the traders were waiting for the promised feast, Captain Mackintosh again went to the platform. Just as he reached it, he saw a single horseman galloping at headlong speed towards the fort, and in the distance, as if pursuing him, he observed an extended line of mounted savages. His heart misgave him on discovering that the fugitive was Le Brun, who, not even casting a glance over his shoulder, made straight for the gate.

Captain Mackintosh hurried down to meet him. "What has happened?" he inquired, with difficulty commanding his voice. "Where are the young ladies and my son?"

"Monsieur, I cannot tell, though I fear the worst," answered Le Brun, throwing himself from his panting horse, which stood covered with foam at the gate. "I was on the track of the young ladies, and Monsieur Norman, when I saw far away a large troop of Indians. I endeavoured to avoid them, but was discovered, and they came thundering across the prairie in pursuit of me. I fled for my life, feeling sure that they would take my scalp, should I be overtaken, and that is all I know. I would have died to save the young ladies, but it was beyond my power to help them."

While he was speaking a shout was heard from one of the Indians, who had remained with the horses outside the gate. In an instant the visitors sprang to their feet, and drawing their tomahawks from beneath their cloaks, uttering similar cries, rushed towards the white men standing round. An athletic savage was about to strike Captain Mackintosh, when a shot, fired by the hump-backed Indian, pierced his heart. Another savage shared the same fate. The remainder fought desperately, their aim evidently being to keep the gate open until the arrival of the approaching horsemen.

The instant the alarm was given several of the garrison, who had remained concealed, appeared from various quarters, and furiously attacking the treacherous Indians, shot several of them down, the remainder being allowed to make their escape through the gate, which was immediately closed and strongly barred behind them.

So rapidly had everything been done that up to this time scarcely a minute had elapsed since Le Brun had entered the fort.

Before it was perceived what he was about to do, the hump-backed Indian had struck his knife into the breasts of those who had fallen, several of whom were still struggling on the ground.

We must now return to the riding party. They cantered gaily on, enjoying the pure fresh air, the exhilarating exercise, and the scenery, notwithstanding that its general features were well known to them. To the south and west extended the level prairies, covered in many places with rich grass, though in others sandy and barren, while to the east rose a ridge of tree-covered hills, through which the river forced its way, bordered by maples, willows, and elms. On the other side of the river the hills swept round, rising almost abruptly from its margin, with here and there small fertile valleys dividing the heights. To the south-east was a lake of some size, also fringed by graceful trees, beyond which appeared another blue distant range, adding much to the picturesque beauty of the landscape. On approaching the northern end of the lake, they saw a splendid flock of pelicans floating on its calm surface, sailing round and round, but as they got nearer, the birds spreading their wings, flew majestically off until they disappeared in the distance. Magpies, grackles, cat birds, and many other of the winged tribe, appeared in considerable numbers among the trees, or disporting themselves on the lake or river.

"It is so long since we have had a gallop, that I vote we take a good long one," exclaimed Norman; and Sybil and Effie, whose spirits had also risen, expressed their readiness to do

W. H. G. Kingston

as he proposed.

"Then let us take the circuit of the lake," said Norman. "I have gone round it several times; and there is plenty of hard ground, though there are some swampy places which it won't do to ride into."

They had, however, not gone far, when Norman, whose horse was higher than those of his sisters, observed in the distance to the south-west a large body of mounted men, whom he knew from their numbers, and the prevailing colour of their ranks, must be Indians.

He pointed them out to his companions, "They are probably bound either for the fort, or are on a hunting expedition to the eastward, but I cannot yet make out in what direction they are going," he observed. "However, I conclude that they are friends, and should they come near us, I will go forward and meet them. It is always better to show that one wishes to be on good terms with the Redskins, and have no fear of them. You girls, however, keep back. Since the lesson Sybil received, it is as well you should not let them see you pale-faces, if you can help it. '

The young ladies laughed, and Norman soon afterwards observing that the horsemen were approaching, dashed forward to meet them as he proposed.

He had got some little way when he saw that the strangers had put their horses to their topmost speed, and he remarked at their head a tall chief who was galloping on, urging his steed by whip and spur.

"I don't like their looks," he thought. "That fellow is very much like Mysticoose. It will be wiser for the girls to keep clear of them."

Turning round, therefore, he rode back as hard as he could go, and as he rejoined Sybil, and Effie, he advised them to give their horses the whip so that they might not risk an encounter with the strangers. On looking round he saw that the latter were coming directly after them.

"On, girls, on!" he cried out. "I wish that we had turned sooner; but our horses are in good wind and we can keep ahead of these fellows, even should they try to overtake us."

Norman's horse was a powerful one: the young ladies being light weights, and accustomed to riding, giving the rein to their steeds they flew over the ground.

Their attendants, who did not like the appearance of the strangers, making good use of whip and spur, managed to keep up with them.

"There's a ford right ahead, across the river; we will make for it," shouted Norman. "We can then keep along the northern bank. It will be much safer than attempting to reach the fort by the direct track, which would bring us close to those fellows."

Towards the ford, therefore, they directed their course. Trusting to the fleetness of their steeds, they had reason to hope that they should keep ahead of their pursuers; for the Indians' horses, though strong and possessed of great endurance, were incapable, they knew, of going at any great speed.

Norman, looking back, however, saw with vexation that the Indian chief, spurring on his animal, was fast distancing most of his followers, somewhat scattered, though not far off. There were several other savages endeavouring to keep up with him. Again and again, Norman urged Sybil and his sister to give the rein to their steeds.

"Never fear. Stick on; the animals won't come down," he shouted.

They both kept up their courage, though fully alive to their dangerous position. Sybil, indeed, suspected that Mysticoose was at the head of the party, and that his object was to capture her. She nerved herself up, however, for whatever might occur.

Though Norman had assured them that there was no risk of their horses falling, she saw, as she approached the river, that the ground was becoming more uneven. Rocks and the stumps of trees, burnt in a recent fire, cropped up here and there, and fallen logs, some so close together that the horses in leaping might stumble over others further off.

Beyond, the ground appeared marshy, and though it might not be too soft for them to get over, they would be delayed until their pursuers had overtaken them.

Still, the girls holding their reins ready to lift their horses should they stumble, continued urging them on with their whips, and Norman, as he looked at them, wondered at their nerve and apparently calm demeanour.

He carried a brace of pistols in his belt, and the two men had their buffalo guns, short weapons, useful for a close encounter, and he resolved to fight to the last rather than let his sister and Sybil be captured. He knew at the same time, how hopeless it would be to contend with their numerous, well-armed enemies.

The rough ground was crossed, the marshy spot was reached, and the horses dashed on, floundering through it, their feet at times sinking so deep that it appeared impossible to draw them out again, while even Norman had to stick tight to keep his seat. He scarcely dared look round, but he fancied that he could hear the clattering of horses hoofs on the hard ground they had just before passed over.

"Hold on!" he shouted, "we shall soon get through the marsh and the savages will find it no easy matter to follow us!"

Though he said this, he knew there was the ford to be crossed, and that could only be done at a walking pace, so that before they could get to the other side, the savages would already have reached the margin of the stream. Once more he turned round.

The chief and half a dozen of his followers were already on the borders of the marsh, some going on one side, some on the other, to find a harder part for crossing.

Happily, however, just then, the young ladies' steeds reached firmer ground, and sprang forward. They were now making directly for the ford, and Norman hoped once more, though almost against hope, that they might get across in time to obtain another good start of their pursuers.

The savages, however, knowing the nature of the ground better than they did, had succeeded in passing it much more rapidly, and Norman saw that in a few minutes they would be up to them. He had almost lost all hope of escape when two horsemen, evidently white men, appeared on the brow of the ridge on the opposite side.

A glance must have shown them the state of affairs, and at the risk of breaking their necks, they came rattling down the steep descent, the horses sometimes sliding almost on their haunches, sometimes leaping forward.

"That is Hector!" cried Norman, recognising his brother; and then the thought occurred to him that he and his companion would share the fate to which it appeared likely they were doomed. Hector and his companion, who, as may be supposed, was Loraine, regardless of the danger into which they were running, dashed forward, and without stopping, plunged into the ford to meet the fugitives, who had all by this time began the passage.

The appearance of only two white men did not deter the Redskins from continuing the pursuit, and having, their guns in their hands, got within thirty yards or so of the two attendants, they fired. Both shots took effect.

One poor fellow fell from his horse; the other, though wounded, clung on still, endeavouring to escape. The Indians came pressing on. One of them, who had got abreast of his chief, attempted to grapple with Hector, and Mysticoose himself was about to seize Sybil, when Loraine, dashing forward and levelling a pistol, shot him in the arm. The limb hung powerless at his side. But notwithstanding, taking the reins in his teeth, the savage chief again attempted with his other hand to take hold of her, while, fearing that she would escape him, he shouted to his followers, who, with fearful shrieks, were pressing on. Her horse, terrified by the sound, bounding forward, she escaped him. Enraged at his failure, he lifted his tomahawk to hurl it at her head, when Loraine with the butt of a pistol struck down his arm; and at that instant a horseman was seen on the top of the ridge. The stranger was old Sass. At a glance he took in the state of affairs. Instead of descending, however, he turned round and shouted loudly in Cree—

"Come on, come on! Here are your enemies, here are your enemies! We've a fine band of them in our power. Quick, quick, or they will escape us!"

Then, as if his followers were close behind, he began to descend almost as rapidly as had the younger men. The Blackfeet, evidently believing that in another minute a large body of their foes would be upon them, turned their horses' heads, and without looking again at the top of the ridge, began a rapid retreat, carrying Mysticoose along with them, their flight hastened by the loud shout which, Hector and Norman setting the example, was raised by the white men.

Norman had not forgotten the poor fellow who had fallen in his defence, and succeeded in catching him as he came to the surface, and dragging him to the shore.

"We must get to the top of the hill and show ourselves, or the Blackfeet may suspect the trick we played them," said old Sass. "That done, we'll ride as fast as our horses' legs can carry us to Fort Duncan. I'll help you with that poor fellow," he added, addressing Norman. "Here, friend, mount your horse; many a man has ridden a score of miles with a worse wound."

The half-breed, knowing that his life depended upon his following the advice, succeeded in getting into his saddle, when the whole party, winding their way up the height, which was of no great elevation, showed themselves on the summit, appearing as if they were the front rank of a body of horsemen about to descend to the river. Such was the idea, in all probability, that the Blackfeet entertained as they were seen in the distance galloping off to the south-west.

The party had to make a considerable circuit, and notwithstanding their wish to hurry forward were compelled frequently to proceed at a foot pace, although they pushed on whenever the ground would allow.

On reaching the top of the hill overlooking the prairie on the southern side of the river, they caught sight of the Blackfeet band in the distance, galloping, it appeared, towards the fort. Whether they themselves were perceived, they could not tell; but Norman fancied that he saw a band separate from the rest, and direct their course towards the river. It would have answered no purpose to stop and ascertain this, though, should such be the case, it was more necessary than ever to gain the fort without delay.

Descending the hill, they pushed forward as before; but Norman cast many an uneasy glance to the left, fearing that the savages might, having swam their horses across the river, pounce suddenly out upon them.

They had got about half-way, when the sound of distant firing reached their ears.

"Where can that come from?" asked Hector, who was riding with his brother.

"From the fort, I am afraid," answered Norman. "The Blackfeet must have attacked it, hoping to get in while some of the garrison are away; but my father will, I trust, have been prepared for them, though I am afraid that some traders, who arrived just before we set off, must have come with treacherous designs, and will try to help their friends outside."

"I thought before this that a fine fellow who came with us— Allan Keith, one of your clerks—would have arrived with a party of half-breeds, whom he expected to enlist," said Hector. "We calculated that he would have been here, as we were greatly delayed on our journey," and he briefly related the adventures Loraine and he had met with.

"Hurrah! Here's a level place. We can push on," cried

Norman; and the party, putting their horses into a gallop, dashed forward. As they did so, rapid firing, echoing among the hills, was again and again heard, evidently coming from the direction of the fort.

W. H. G. Kingston

CHAPTER SEVEN

The glowing sun was touching the line where the blue sky and prairie met, his rays casting a ruddy hue over the calm surface of the river, when the party, conducted by Norman, reached the northern bank opposite the fort, they having been delayed by attending to the wounded man, who could with difficulty be brought along. As they descended the slope to the river they caught sight of a body of horsemen galloping away across the prairie. Norman, as he watched them, was certain that they were the savages who had pursued his party.

"Thank Heaven, the Redskins have been defeated!" exclaimed Hector; "but had it not been for the warning you sent my father, friend Sass, the case might have been very different."

Norman now hailed at the top of his voice for a boat.

In a short time two men were seen launching one from a shed close to the water. They quickly brought her across. As she would not carry the whole of the party, the two young ladies, and, at their request, the wounded men, were first ferried over.

Captain Mackintosh stood on the bank to receive them, and, as Sybil and Effie threw themselves into his arms, their feelings at length giving way, they burst into tears.

"There is nothing more to fear; we have driven off the Blackfeet, and they have received a lesson which they will not soon forget, I trust," he said.

He then inquired how they had been preserved. They were both eloquent in describing the way Hector and Loraine, with their old companion, had rescued them; but there was no time to say much just then. While some of the garrison, who had come down for the purpose, carried the wounded men into the fort, the rest of the party were ferried across the river. Captain Mackintosh gave a fatherly greeting to Hector, who then introduced Loraine.

"I have to thank you, sir, for the brave way in which you saved this young lady from the clutches of the savage chief. Had it not been for your gallantry, she might have been carried off. As the fellow has, however escaped, we must still keep careful watch for her protection."

Loraine expressed himself appropriately, saying how rejoiced he was to have been of service, and that it made ample amends to him for his disappointment in not having arrived in time to warn Captain Mackintosh of the Indians' plot to surprise the fort.

Old Sass, who had modestly kept out of the way, now came in for his share of thanks; and the whole garrison, when they heard of the clever way in which he had frightened off the Blackfeet, were enthusiastic in their expressions of admiration at his conduct. The hump-backed Indian, who, as may be supposed, was no other than Greensnake, was also made much of, all acknowledging that it was through the warning he had brought that they were put on their guard against the intended treachery of their cunning enemies.

The bodies of the Indians, and other signs of the strife, had been removed before the party had entered the fort. The young ladies at once disappeared into the house, under charge of Mrs Mackintosh, whose maternal feelings had been fearfully tried during their absence. They did not appear again until the evening, when Hector declared that they looked as blooming as ever.

Loraine soon won the regard of Captain Mackintosh and Norman. Every hour the young Englishman remained in the society of the original of the beautiful picture he so much admired, endeared her more and more to him; and it is not surprising that a girl who had seen so few gentlemen, except her brothers and some of the Hudson's Bay clerks, should have given him her heart in return. Loraine was not a man to trifle with a girl's affections, and sooner than he might otherwise have done, he expressed his wishes to Captain Mackintosh.

"I conclude Hector has told you that Sybil is not my daughter, though she is as dear to me as if she were," answered Captain Mackintosh. "I am, in truth, utterly ignorant of her parentage. Soon after my marriage, while quartered in Upper Canada, my wife and I made an excursion through Lake Ontario and the Sault Sainte Marie to the shores of Lake Superior. We intended proceeding across the lake to the then wild region of the west.

"While staying at a small cottage on the north side of the falls of Sainte Marie, the very day before we were to sail, a heavy gale came on. As we were unable to embark, not to disappoint my wife, I proposed to make an excursion, partly on foot and partly on horseback, as far as we could proceed along the north shore of the lake to Groscap, a conical hill which we could see rising to a considerable elevation in the distance. We found the path far more difficult than we had expected, and at length, our object unaccomplished, we turned our steps homeward. We had not got far when the rain began to come down in torrents, and we were glad to take shelter in a log hut of the roughest description, built on some rising ground a short way from the shore of the lake. It was unoccupied, but as there was a hearth and chimney, we directed our attendants to obtain some fuel and lighted a fire to dry our drenched garments. In vain we waited for the weather to clear. Darkness coming on, we found that we must spend the night in the hut, not a pleasant prospect, but it was preferable to making our way through the forest with the rain pouring down on our heads.

"The wind howled and whistled, the waves dashed furiously against the shore, the trees bent and writhed beneath the blast, and my fear was that some of those surrounding the hut might be uprooted and crush in the roof. I went frequently to the door, in the hopes of discovering a rent in the clouds which might enable me to hold out some prospect to my wife of the cessation of the storm. While looking up at the sky I fancied that I heard the plaintive cry of a child. The next moment I thought that it must be that of some wild animal, and was about to re-enter the hut when it was repeated. Telling my wife what I was about to do, I desired the two men to accompany me, and groped my way through the darkness in the direction whence the sound had come. Again I heard the cry, and, guided by it, I almost stumbled over a woman lying on the ground, with a child in her arms. The woman was speechless, but was uttering low moans. I took the child in my arms and hurried back to the hut, while the men followed me, conveying the almost inanimate form of the woman.

"'Heaven has sent us here to rescue the little creature,' exclaimed my wife, as I put the infant in her arms.

W. H. G. Kingston

"She lost no time in taking off its wet clothes and wrapping it up in a shawl.

"'It is a little girl,' she said, 'and I trust has received no injury. We must attend to the poor mother,' she added, as the men brought in the body of the woman and laid her before the blazing fire. 'Why, she cannot be the mother of this child; she is an Indian, and the child is beautifully fair,' exclaimed my wife, as, giving me the baby, she knelt down by the side of the woman to try and restore her to animation. All her efforts, however, were in vain. Before many minutes had past she had breathed her last. We took off some of the few ornaments she wore about her dress, to assist us in identifying her, and the men then placed the body at the further end of the hut.

"We had, as you may suppose, no sleep that night; my wife, indeed, was fully occupied in nursing the baby. Providentially I had brought, instead of wine, a bottle of milk for my wife, very little of which she had drank, and with this she was happily able to feed the child.

"How the woman and child had come to be in the position in which we had found them, I could not tell; but our guides asserted that they must have escaped from a wrecked canoe, and possibly others of the party might have got safe on shore and would be able to tell us to whom the child belonged.

"When morning came the storm cleared off, and though my wife was anxious to get back to our lodgings, I set off to explore the beach with one of our guides. We went a considerable distance in both directions, but no one could we discover, nor a trace of a canoe or boat of any sort. If the woman had escaped therefore, as we supposed, from a canoe, it must have foundered or been knocked to pieces on the rocks, and the fragments and bodies of those on board have been driven far out again on the lake.

"After our vain search, we commenced our journey, my wife carrying the little girl in her arms. On our way we called at the Hudson's Bay Company's post, situated above the falls, where the hospitable superintendent begged us to remain, and offered to take care of the child until its friends could be discovered. My wife, however, refused to part with her treasure-trove, as she called the little foundling, and so strongly expressed her wish to adopt her, that, having none of our own, I consented, provided no relative appeared to claim her. On seeing the ornaments which we had taken from the Indian woman, the superintendent pronounced them to be those worn by Crees, and thought by their means he might discover the child's relatives.

"He at once sent to the hut to bury the poor woman, and we remained at our cottage until we could receive the information our friend promised to obtain. He had not expected any canoe from the west, and could not account for the one which was supposed to be lost.

"We waited on, but as the superintendent of the post could obtain no information in the neighbourhood, and told us that it might be many months before he could get any from the Far West, whence there could be little doubt the canoe had come, we returned to Toronto with the child. She became our adopted daughter, and from that day to this, notwithstanding all our inquiries, we have been unable to learn her parentage. Though we soon afterwards had a child of our own, she ever retained the same hold on our affections which she had at first enjoyed."

"I cannot but suppose that so lovely a creature must be of gentle birth," exclaimed Loraine; "but whether she is or not, with your leave, if she consents to be mine, I will marry her as soon as a clergyman can be found to unite us."

"Although we shall all be sorry to part from her, I will throw no obstacle in the way of what may tend to her happiness as well as yours," answered Captain Mackintosh, shaking Loraine by the hand.

As it may be supposed, the young lover felt pretty sure of the answer Sybil would give him, nor was he mistaken.

Norman and Hector looked somewhat grave.

"And so you intend to carry off Sybil," exclaimed the latter. "I almost wish that I hadn't brought you to the fort, old fellow. But one good thing is that you cannot take her away until you are married, and you may have to wait a long time for that."

Effie felt the expected parting with Sybil more than any one else. She was also anxious, and as much out of spirits as it seemed possible for so happy a creature to be, for Hector had naturally told her that Allan Keith had gone to obtain reinforcements for the garrison of the fort, and had expressed his surprise that they had not long before this arrived.

On his first arrival a room had been assigned to Isaac Sass, and he had been invited to the captain's table, when, notwithstanding his rough appearance, he showed that he was a man of good education, though ignorant of the events which had of late taken place in the world. He generally sat opposite to Sybil, and it was remarked that his eyes were often fixed intently on her, but that he withdrew them whenever he saw that he was observed. He would follow her about the fort, or when she went out to walk in its immediate neighbourhood, as if wishing to watch over her safety, and when he occasionally addressed her his voice assumed a softness contrasting greatly with the somewhat harsh tone in which he ordinarily spoke.

"If ever angels come on earth, that sweet sister of yours is one of them," he remarked to Hector one day, while he stood watching Sybil at a distance.

"I will tell her what you say," answered Hector, laughing. "And I'll ask her if she is really one. Perhaps she may be, for, do you know that she is not my sister?" and Hector told him the story of her discovery.

Isaac Sass made no reply, but seemed to be pondering deeply on what he had heard.

He continued to watch Sybil with even greater interest than before, and managed to obtain from Captain Mackintosh a confirmation of the account Hector had given him. He said nothing, however, in reply; but his manner showed that he was laying some restraint on himself, during the remainder of the time he remained at Fort Duncan.

Although Captain Mackintosh paid him every attention, grateful to him for the service he had rendered, the old man, however, appeared at length to grow weary of inactivity, and began to speak of taking his departure with Greensnake for the north.

"It is seldom nowadays that I come near the country of the Blackfeet," he said, addressing Captain Mackintosh. "It may be a long time before you see me here again. It may be I shall never return; but I shall often think of the time I spent with you and your English friends."

Before, however, old Isaac took his departure two horsemen were seen approaching the fort from the westward. Their steeds, as they came to the gate, showed that they had ridden hard. One was a white man and the other an Indian. The first dismounted and entered the gate.

"My name is Harvey," he said, shaking hands with Captain Mackintosh, who advanced to meet him. "I am in charge of the missionary station at White Fish Lake, and have come to ask your assistance for my people, whom the Blackfeet have threatened to destroy. I have felt it my duty to obtain, if possible, the means of protecting them."

"I am well acquainted with your name," answered Captain Mackintosh, who knew Mr Harvey to be a devoted Christian man, one of those brave pioneers of Christianity who, in obedience to the commands of our blessed Lord, have, with their lives in their hands, ventured into the wilds among the savage races of the Far West to win precious souls for Him.

"I would gladly help you," he answered, "but this fort has only lately been attacked, and I should not be justified in weakening the garrison by sending away any of my people. I will, however, thankfully receive you and your family, and those of your flock whom you may wish to bring with you, while the others move northward beyond the reach of their enemies. Even were I to spare you half a dozen men, they would be of little use in repelling an attack of the daring Blackfeet."

"I feel that you are right, and that I must remove my family, and leave our house and garden to be destroyed," answered Mr Harvey. "Pray do not misunderstand me, and suppose that I mistrust God's protecting care; but I know that He would have us take all reasonable measures for our safety, and fly from earthly, as he directs us to escape from spiritual, foes."

"We will discuss the matter after you have rested, and I have had time to think it over," answered Captain Mackintosh. "It is my private wish as well as my public duty to afford every assistance in my power to missionaries labouring among the Indians, and you may depend on my doing all I justly can to afford you the aid you wish. However, I now advise you to lie down and rest while some food is preparing."

Mr Harvey acknowledged that he was very tired, and gratefully accepted the offer, before paying his respects to the ladies of the family.

Sybil looked somewhat confused when she heard that a clergyman had arrived at the fort.

"You need not be alarmed," said Effie, somewhat slily. "From what papa says, he can only remain a few hours. He has to hurry back to his station, and declines remaining even one night."

What might have been Loraine's wish need not be said, but Mr Harvey promised, should his life be spared, to return shortly to perform the ceremony which was to make Sybil his.

Captain Mackintosh, after reflecting, agreed to send five of his men, under the orders of Le Brun, to protect Mr Harvey's station, for he guessed that, without the prospect of booty, notwithstanding their threats, the Blackfeet would not venture to attack it, even though opposed by so small a number; for, if successful, they would gain but little, and would be certain to lose several men.

Le Brun, a brave fellow, laughed at the notion.

Just as Mr Harvey was about to set out, old Sass and

Greensnake appeared mounted at the gate.

"I'll go with you, friend," he said, addressing the clergyman. "Though I've not had much to do with parsons in my day, I want to have a talk with you, and maybe if those villains, the Blackfeet, try to give you any trouble, I may be of as much use as those six men you are taking with muskets and pistols."

Before finally starting, the old man bade adieu to Captain Mackintosh and his family, as also to Loraine.

He gazed in Sybil's face as he took her hand. "I have not prayed for many a day, but if God will hear the prayers of such an outcast as I am, I will ask Him to bless you and make you happy with the noble young Englishman to whom you have given your heart. It is my belief that he will prove true and faithful."

He spoke in a similar strain to Loraine; and turning, with an evident effort, to where Greensnake was holding his horse, mounted, and joined Mr Harvey, who had already left the fort.

CHAPTER EIGHT

Life in a fort in the Far West is not as monotonous as may be supposed. There is a variety of work to be done. The hunters are employed in procuring buffalo, deer, and other game for provisions during the many winter months. The meat has to be preserved in summer by being converted into pemmican, and in winter by being placed in deep pits, with floors of ice between each intervening layer of meat, and then covered up with snow. When the fort is in the neighbourhood of a lake or river, fish have to be caught and preserved. This is done by salting them in summer, and freezing them as soon as the cold becomes intense enough. Numerous horses have to be attended to, and dogs trained for dragging the sleighs when the snow covers the ground, the only mode then possible of travelling. Sleighs, carts, snow-shoes, and harness of all sorts, have to be manufactured, and moccasins and winter clothing prepared. In the neighbourhood of some forts gardens containing vegetables, and fields of maize, wheat, and oats have to be attended to. In others boats and canoes are built, while at all the gunsmith has constant work in repairing damaged fire-arms.

Trappers are constantly coming and going, bringing peltries, buffalo, deer, and wolf-skins, as well as other produce of the chase. Some are half-breeds, others white men, but the greater number pure Indians. Some arrive with several bales,

W. H. G. Kingston

others only bring a few skins to exchange for powder and shot, and a new trap or two. Then the skins obtained have to be sorted, repacked, and despatched either to York factory in the north, or to Fort Garry in the south; while stores and provisions at certain periods arrive, and the men transporting them have to be entertained until they are ready to return to head-quarters.

Such was the existence which the inmates of Fort Duncan were leading. Under other circumstances Loraine might soon have grown tired of so limited a sphere of action, but every day he became more and more attached—if that were possible—to Sybil; and although he had intended to perform the journey across the Rocky Mountains to Vancouver's Island, he could not bring himself to leave her exposed to dangers such as those from which she had lately been preserved.

Sybil had no wish to let him go, for though short as was the time since they had first met, he had become all in all to her; and no wonder when Hector, who had opportunities of knowing him well, declared that he was one of the finest, noblest, best fellows he had ever fell in with, right-minded, true and brave; and Sybil was convinced that this account was not exaggerated.

Next to Loraine, Hector's chief friend was Allan Keith, whom he considered almost the equal of the first. He had become very anxious at the non-appearance of Allan and the half-breed hunters he had hoped to enlist. Either he must have failed in inducing them to accompany him, or he had encountered some hostile Indians on the way, which was not very likely, or had been compelled to make a wide circuit to avoid them. At last Hector asked his father's permission to take two or three men with him, and to travel northward in the direction Keith would most likely come, in the hopes of falling in with him, and giving assistance should it be required. "He may have met with some such misadventure as Loraine and I did; or he may have expended his ammunition and be starving," he observed.

Effie was very grateful to Hector when she heard of his proposal.

"I won't ask you to accompany me, Loraine," he said to his friend, "for I suspect that Sybil would greatly object to your going away; and as you are less accustomed to the style of life than our men, you would knock up sooner than they would. I wish that old Sass had been here with his boy Greensnake; they would, by some means or other, have discovered him, wherever he is."

Loraine made no reply. He certainly had no wish to go, and he agreed with Hector that the hunters were more accustomed to the style of life they would have to lead than he was; still, in his anxiety to assist Keith, he was ready to sacrifice much, but if a sufficient number of men from the fort could be spared, his aid would not be required.

To Hector's disappointment, however, Captain Mackintosh objected to his taking any men from the fort.

"The best hunters are required to go out in search of game, and the garrison is already weakened by those who have accompanied Mr Harvey," he remarked. "Although I am as anxious as you are about Keith, yet duty compels me to refuse your request, and I cannot let you go alone, or even with one man. Had Le Brun been here I might have sent him, as he is worth two or three others; but unless Mr Harvey abandons his station and takes refuge in the fort, it may be some time before he returns, and I hope before then we shall either see or hear of Keith."

Still Hector did not abandon his plan. Norman was ready to go; and Loraine, when he found that no one else could be spared, without consulting Sybil, volunteered to accompany him.

Captain Mackintosh finding that his sons were so bent on the expedition, and that their guest was ready to sacrifice his own inclination, on further considering the matter, gave his consent, and agreed to send one of the best hunters and guides with them, provided they promised not to be absent more than ten days, and to leave behind them marks by which their trail could be followed up.

Effie thanked Loraine warmly; and even Sybil acknowledged that as he was going from a generous motive, she could not venture to ask him to stay behind.

The undertaking being determined on, the party rapidly made their preparations. Having crossed the river where the horses were waiting for them, they set out. Besides those they rode, each person had a spare horse on which were carried a few light articles required for camping.

Sybil and Effie stood on the ramparts facing the river, and bade them adieu, as they wound their way up the hill on the opposite bank.

Effie felt happier than she had been for some time; and it was now her part to console Sybil for Loraine's absence, assuring her that the party would not return without bringing tidings of Allan.

Several of the hunters had been out for three days in search of buffalo. They were expected back that night; but as they did not make their appearance, the gates were closed as usual, and sentries posted to keep watch at night.

Towards morning the man on duty in one of the towers, saw through the gloom a horseman coming at full speed towards the fort.

"Vite, vite, open the gate; I am well-nigh done for," he shouted. "The rest have been killed, and I have had a hard matter to escape from the savages."

The sentry gave the alarm, the gates were opened, and Jacques Robe, one of the hunters, rode in. He almost fell from his horse into the arms of two of the men who had hastened out to meet him. An arrow was in his side, and he was bleeding from other wounds.

The gates being closed, Captain Mackintosh directed the wounded man to be carried to his house, and as soon as he had sent the garrison to the ramparts to be ready should the enemy appear, he hastened to attend to him.

The poor fellow's wounds though severe were not likely to prove mortal. The arrow was extracted by sawing off the head, the other hurts being bound up, the bullets having happily not lodged in his body. Captain Mackintosh then left his patient to the care of his wife and went out to make further arrangements for the defence. He now regretted having allowed his sons and Loraine to go away, contrary to his better judgment. They could not, however, as yet have got to any distance; and as their assistance would be of the greatest value he resolved at once to recall them. He hoped that they would be able to return in time to assist in the defence of the fort, as probably the Blackfeet, knowing that notice would be given of their approach by the escape of Jacques Robe, would not venture to attack it, if such was their intention, until the following night. He therefore ordered Jules Buffet, an active and intelligent scout, to cross the river and hasten as fast as his horse would carry him after

W. H. G. Kingston

the party.

"They will not hesitate about returning when they hear what is likely to occur," he observed.

Jules, stuffing some pemmican and bread into his pouch, without loss of a moment set off.

It was still too dark to observe his movements; but the man who had gone to assist him in catching and saddling his horse, reported that he had started in safety, and that knowing the country, in spite of the obscurity, he would have no difficulty in carrying out his instructions.

Captain Mackintosh laid strict injunctions on Sybil and his wife and daughter, on no account to leave the shelter of the house, observing, "It will become still darker than it is at present before day breaks, and it is possible that during the time the savages may take the opportunity of sending a shower of arrows into the fort. With our reduced numbers, I must not venture to send out scouts to ascertain their position; they may be still at a distance, or they may be creeping up towards the fort hoping to take us by surprise."

The ladies exhibited the courage that might have been expected of them when they, without fear, came to live in that remote fort, situated, as they well knew, in the neighbourhood of hostile tribes.

Mrs Mackintosh got lint and bandages and cordials ready, in case any of the garrison should be wounded.

Captain Mackintosh then went round the fort to encourage the scanty garrison, and to see that they were on the watch. He endeavoured to pierce the gloom, but could distinguish no objects moving on the prairie. Still, he knew well the various tricks to which the Redskins were likely to resort. They might be close by, creeping up on hands and knees among the grass, or along the bank of the river so as to attack the fort at the real as well as in front. He prepared for both contingencies, posting careful men at every assailable point.

The minutes went slowly by. He greatly missed his sons, and Loraine, who would have been of essential service in watching the more dangerous points. Le Brun, a most trustworthy man, was away, and two of his best hunters and scouts had been killed, while another lay wounded and useless. Still he endeavoured to make up for the limited number of his men by his own energy and watchfulness.

As he hurried round and round, he praised those who were most on the alert, and warned the others of the dangers of negligence. He more than once went down to examine his watch, and ascertain how the time was passing, for of course no lights were shown on the ramparts, and then again he hurried up to look over the prairie.

At length a bright streak appeared across the eastern sky. The light increased, and it was with a sigh of heart-felt relief, when at last, being able to see across the prairie, he discovered that not a single object was moving over its broad expanse.

"It is as I thought, then," he said to himself; "the Blackfeet have deemed it prudent not to show themselves until they can catch us off our guard. We shall have, I trust, a day's rest, and by the evening my boys and their brave friends will have returned; and even should poor Keith have met with disaster, Burnett may send us reinforcements from Edmonton. I pray that the savages have not paid a visit to Harvey's station, or it may have gone hard with him. Now I may go down and console Mrs Mackintosh and the girls, and get some

W. H. G. Kingston

breakfast;" and the gallant Captain, having again charged the sentries to keep on the alert, returned to his house.

The day wore on, and had it not been for Jacques Robe's positive assertion that he had escaped from an unusually large body of Blackfeet, it might have been supposed that there was no cause for alarm.

Not even a buffalo or deer appeared. That, however, was not unusual; indeed, the only cause to create suspicion was that no traders, either Indians or others, arrived at the fort.

Noon had passed, and had Jules Buffet ridden as fast as he proposed, Loraine and his companions might soon return. Still they did not appear.

Sybil and Effie frequently went to the southern platform to look out, but returned each time disappointed.

Captain Mackintosh, who had gone to the top of the look-out tower, swept with his telescope the horizon to the south and west, towards which the glowing sun was once more sinking.

As he looked, he fancied that he could detect objects moving above the tall grass, embrowned with the tints of autumn. If they were Indians they probably did not suppose that they could be discovered at so great a distance. They might, indeed, have been only a herd of deer scampering across the plain. Still, as he looked again and again through his glass, he fancied that he could distinguish the plumed heads and shoulders of Indian warriors.

"They shall not catch us napping, at all events," he said to himself; "and I trust to Heaven to enable us to make good use of the means at our disposal."

He was unwilling to leave his post, while there was sufficient daylight to give him a chance of ascertaining whether the objects he saw were mounted Indians or not: he knew that at such a distance men on foot could not possibly be seen. He had much less to fear from men on horseback than from the stealthy approach of savages on foot, who might creep up almost unperceived close to the walls.

At length the increasing shadows of evening shrouded the view, and he made another round to warn the sentries, as before, to be on the alert, telling them that they might expect to be attacked before morning.

Just as he reached the river side of the platform, he heard a shout. It was Norman's voice, asking for a boat to be sent over.

He immediately, therefore, ordered two of the men usually employed in the service to pull across, and in a short time his sons and Loraine entered the fort. It need not be said that they were welcomed by those who had been so long looking for them. Jules Buffet had fulfilled his promise by pushing forward at full speed, and had overtaken them just as his horse fell utterly exhausted, while they were making their noon-day halt. They had galloped back on fresh horses, which at the end of the ride seemed scarcely able to stand.

"But we have managed it," cried Hector, "and now I hope the Redskins won't disappoint us. I wish, however, that we could have brought Allan Keith; but we met with no signs of him or his party, and he may be still a hundred miles away or more."

The addition of five persons in whom he could trust, made Captain Mackintosh hope more than ever that he should be able successfully to resist the expected attack of the

Blackfeet. That they would come that night he felt almost certain, as also that the great object of their young chief Mysticoose was to carry off Sybil. He had, however, probably induced his people to undertake the expedition by promising them the pillage of the fort. They had a few years before this surprised Bow Fort, which afforded them a rich booty, and they might naturally expect to succeed in capturing Fort Duncan, which was not better provided with the means of defence. Never, however, before the recent attempt of Mysticoose to take it by treachery, had it been attacked.

The fresh arrivals, after taking some food, lay down to get the rest they so much required, Captain Mackintosh promising to call them should any signs of the approaching enemy be discovered. Each man on the ramparts was provided with a lantern, kept shaded until required, to throw a light on the ground round the fort, which, as was rightly expected, would tend greatly to disconcert the assailants, should they creep up with the expectation of effecting a surprise.

Hour after hour went by.

"They intend, I suspect, as I thought they would yesterday morning, to make their attack a short time before daylight, when they fancy we shall be weary with watching, and off our guard," observed Captain Mackintosh to Loraine, who had joined him on the platform.

"Then we may expect them before long," said Loraine, looking at his watch by the light of a lantern.

Scarcely had he spoken, than an arrow flew between him and Captain Mackintosh. He had just time to shout to his people to get under cover, when a whole flight came whistling over their heads, followed by a terrific war whoop, the most fearful sound of which the human voice is capable.

The men in the garrison shouted in return, several of them well accustomed to the noise giving vent to derisive laughter.

"The painted savages fancy that we are to be frightened by yells like yon," cried Sandy Macpherson, an old Scotchman, who had been since his youth in the service of the company. "They may shoot their arrows and shout as loud as they like, but it won't help them to get inside the fort, lads, I ken. Wait till we can see their heads, and then send a shower of bullets among them, but dinna fire till the captain gives the word, an' then blaze away as fast as ye can load."

"Bravo, Sandy! That's just what we must do," cried Hector, who was passing at the moment, having been sent round by his father to see that the men were at their proper stations.

A shout from Sandy, of "There they are!" and the word to fire, produced a blaze of light round the fort.

The Blackfeet, many of whom had muskets, fired in return, and then countless dark forms were seen dashing forward, some to attempt to scale the walls, others to force open the gate.

CHAPTER NINE

So resolutely carried on was the attack of the Indians, that Captain Mackintosh could not help fearing that it must succeed. Two of his men had been killed, and both his sons were wounded, although they refused to retire, and continued firing through the loop-holed walls. The fiercest attack was made on the gate, which Mysticoose evidently hoped to break open, and to force his way in. Loraine undertook to defend it to the last. Captain Mackintosh, knowing that he would do so, was able to turn his attention to other points.

Notwithstanding the desperate manner in which they came on to the attack, the assailants were kept at bay; but so much powder had at length been expended, that Captain Mackintosh found to his dismay that the stock was running short.

"We must manage to hold out until daylight, and then, through Heaven's mercy, the savages may be induced to give up the attempt," he observed to Sandy, who brought him the alarming information.

"Ay, sir, that we will; and when the powder is done, we will take to our pikes and bayonets. The Redskins will have no mind to face them."

The savage chief seemed resolved, however, to succeed. Again and again he and his followers rushed up to the gate, which they assailed with their axes, hewing at the stout wood in the expectation of cutting it through. Many fell in the attempt by the hot fire kept up on them from either side.

At last they were driven back, and the garrison gave vent to a loud cheer, confident that the enemy were about to take to flight.

For a short interval the fighting ceased; but the savages, urged by Mysticoose, again came on, this time to make another effort to scale the palisades. Some stood on the backs of their companions, trying to reach the summit; others tugged away at the stout timbers, endeavouring to pull them down; but they resisted all their efforts.

The defenders of the fort rushed here and there, striking fierce blows with their axes wherever an Indian showed himself, thrusting with their pikes, and hurling back their assailants. Still, it was too likely that numbers would prevail. On either side the Indians were swarming up, and one man had often to contend with a dozen before others of the defenders could come to his assistance. Several more of the garrison had been wounded; but no one, while he had strength to wield a weapon, retired from his post. At last the Indians, finding that so many of their party had fallen, and that, in spite of all their efforts, they were unable to climb over the palisades, desisted from the attempt, and again retired out of gunshot. Though they could not be seen, their voices were heard on three sides of the fort, showing that they had not altogether abandoned the attempt.

"I wonder what they will do next?" said Hector to his brother. "Do you think they have had enough of it?"

"If that fellow Mysticoose has escaped, I'm afraid he'll urge them to come on again," answered Norman. "It still wants an hour to daylight, and they are up to some trick or other, you may depend upon that. Perhaps they are creeping round to try and get in at the rear of the fort by climbing up on that side, thinking that we should not guard it so carefully as the front. Come along, let us try and find out what they are about."

They accordingly hurried up to the ramparts overlooking the river; but when they peered down through the gloom, they could see nothing moving. They urged the men on guard to keep a watchful look-out.

"No fear about our doing that," was the answer. "The Redskins have had enough of climbing over for the present. They are more likely again to try and beat down the gate."

Still the shouts and shrieks in the distance continued.

Hector and Norman returned to their posts in front. They had scarcely got there when Hector's sharp eyes perceived some dark objects moving along the ground. He would have taken them, under other circumstances, for a herd of buffalo, so shapeless did they seem.

He immediately warned the rest of the garrison. The objects came nearer and nearer. It was evident that they were men carrying loads on their backs, who, bounding on before a fire could be opened on them, got close up to the gates at the foot of the palisades. The next instant a number of Indians were observed making off at full speed. They were fired at; but so rapid were their movements, that most of them effected their escape without being hit.

Scarcely had the firing ceased, than small flames were seen

rising out of the loads left close to the fort, which it was now discovered were faggots, brought by the savages for the purpose of burning down the palisades.

Loraine, on seeing this, volunteered to head a party to drag away the faggots before the flames should have time to blaze up; but just as he was about to set out, and the gates were being opened, some more Indians, protected by a band of horsemen, were seen approaching, laden with an additional supply of faggots, with which, using them as shields, they endeavoured to protect themselves from the fire of the garrison. But by this time many of the men, having only a round or two of ammunition remaining, were unwilling to expend it, and the savages as before escaped with slight loss.

"The faggots may blaze up, my boys," cried Captain Mackintosh; "but it will take some time to burn down our palisades." His heart, however, began to sink, as he thought that too probably the enemy would succeed in their design.

Loraine, seeing the fearful danger to which the fort was exposed, again offered to rush out at the head of a party of men, and endeavour to drag away the burning branches. There was a risk, however, that while they were so engaged, the enemy might make a rush for the gate. Already the flames were ascending. As they burned brightly, their glare would expose him and his followers to view. Still, the position of affairs required that the risk, great as it was, should be run. Dense volumes of smoke were coming through the interstices of the palisades, and the circle of flame which rose up round the fort showed that no time must be lost.

Captain Mackintosh sent those who had most ammunition to fire away at the enemy, should they approach. The gates were opened, and Loraine, with his followers, issued forth armed with pikes, to drag away the burning mass. Those at the gate were soon hurled to a distance. They then began to labour away at those spots where the greatest danger was threatened to the palisades.

So rapid were their movements that it was some time before their object was discovered by the Indians, who, however, at length perceived what they were about, and, uttering a war whoop, came rushing towards them.

In vain the party from above endeavoured to keep the savages in check. Loraine ran a fearful risk of being cut off.

Captain Mackintosh, seeing the danger to which he was exposed, shouted to him to retire, while the men within stood ready to close the gates the moment he and his companions had entered. Although warned that the enemy were drawing near, he laboured on to the last, when, turning round, he saw, by the light of the flames, the savages, with tomahawks uplifted, scarcely a dozen paces from him.

His first impulse was to stop and encounter Mysticoose; but by so doing he would delay, he knew, the closing of the gate, and the savages might succeed in entering.

A tomahawk whirled by his head. In another moment he would have a dozen enemies upon him. He sprang back after his companion, and the gate was closed against their assailants, who at once, to wreak their vengeance, began to throw back the blazing faggots against it.

A few shots were fired at the enemy, and then not a single report was heard. Every grain of powder in the fort had been expended.

The Blackfeet had in the mean time been collecting a fresh

supply of faggots, and now, finding themselves unmolested, brought them up to the stockades. At length the stout gate, having caught fire, showed signs of giving way, while the forked flames appeared in all directions between the palisades. In vain the bold hunters sprang here and there with buckets of water—for the fort was well supplied—and dashed it against the burning timbers. It was too evident that ere long the whole front of the fort would be one mass of fire.

"Never fear, lads," cried old Sandy Macpherson, as he saw to a certainty what would happen. "Even when the walls come down, the Redskins won't be in a hurry to make their way over them. We may still keep the 'varmints' at bay for a good time longer, and then just take shelter in the big house, and they'll no get into that in a hurry, while we make good play with our pikes and bayonets."

If Sandy did not forget that the savages, as soon as they got into the inner part of the fort, would set fire to the buildings, he thought it prudent not to say so.

In the mean time, Loraine began to fear that notwithstanding the heroic efforts he and his companions were making, the helpless ones, whom they were ready to sacrifice their lives to protect, would fall into the power of the savages. Language, indeed, cannot describe his feelings. Rather would he have seen his beautiful Sybil dead than carried off by the Indian. "Would it not be possible to get through the back of the fort, and to place the ladies in the boat, then either to carry them down the river, or enable them to make their escape to the northward?" he asked of Captain Mackintosh. "Surely it would be safer than defending them in the house."

"I much fear that the savages, though we do not see them, are

W. H. G. Kingston

watching the banks, and that the attempt would be unsuccessful; yet, as a last resource, we must try it," answered Captain Mackintosh. "I will commit them to your charge."

Loraine's feelings prompted him eagerly to accept the office, and yet, influenced by a high motive, he replied—

"I would propose that your sons should escort them. They are well acquainted with the navigation of the river, and would be more likely to find their way across the country than I should."

"My boys and I must remain at our posts and defend the fort to the last," said Captain Mackintosh. "You must go, my friend. We have but a short time to prepare. Old Sandy shall accompany you. The boat will hold no more. Go on, and let my wife and poor girls know what we have decided, and I will make the required arrangements."

"I will do as you desire," answered Loraine.

In building the fort, the timbers had been so placed that an opening could easily be formed on such an emergency as now occurred. Captain Mackintosh, summoning Sandy, they together removed part of the wood-work. Sandy was about to step through the opening, when he hurriedly drew back, and replacing the timbers exclaimed—

"The Redskins have found us out. I saw half a score of them creeping along the bank. Quick, quick, captain, and stop up the gap!"

All hope of enabling the ladies to escape as he proposed had to be abandoned, and Captain Mackintosh, with a sad heart, leaving Sandy to watch the spot, went back to tell them of the impossibility of carrying out their projected plan.

Scarcely had he reached the building than the towers on either side of the gate, which were blazing furiously, and a large portion of the front, fell down outwards with a loud crash.

A fearful yell of exultation was uttered by the savages, but the encircling flames and the burning timbers still kept them at bay. In a short time, however, the flames would burn out, and they might spring over the smouldering logs.

Disheartened by the desperate way in which their attacks had been met, and not aware that the garrison were destitute of ammunition, they kept at a distance, feeling confident that their prey could not escape them.

As the flames decreased, Captain Mackintosh ordered the men to retreat into the two chief buildings, urging them to hold out bravely to the last. He feared, however, with too much reason, that although they might prolong their resistance, their ultimate destruction was inevitable. Every moment the flames in front were decreasing, although on either side they were creeping along the stockades, threatening everything with speedy destruction.

The savages, hovering round, had been waiting for the moment when they might force their way over the burning ruins. It came at last. Again uttering their fearful war whoops, they came rushing on, confident of success, when a cheer was heard from the left, followed by a rattling fire of musketry. The fierce warriors turned and fled. Their chief himself, who was distinguished by his tall figure and waving plume, was seen to fall. Some of his followers endeavoured to lift him from the ground, but fled with the rest, and in another minute a large body of horsemen galloped up, who were seen, as the glare of the burning stockades fell on them, to be mostly half-breed hunters, led by a white man.

W. H. G. Kingston

"Hurrah! Hurrah! It's Allan Keith," cried Hector, who had been on the look-out through one of the barricaded windows.

In an instant the door was thrown open. The men of the garrison rushed to the burning walls, some with axes to cut them down, others with buckets of water to extinguish the flames.

While the half-breeds were pursuing the flying foe, another party appeared on the right, and in a short time Dr McCrab and Dan Maloney, who had led them, were heartily greeting Captain Mackintosh and his companions, and congratulating them on their narrow escape.

"Faith, my boy, I'm mighty glad that we've come just in the nick of time, and that we shouldn't have done, I'm after thinking, if it hadn't been for falling in with old Isaac Sass, and his impish follower, Master Greensnake," exclaimed Maloney, as he shook Hector's hand. "He told us if we wanted to save you, to put our best feet foremost while he showed us the course to take. It's my belief, too, that he afterwards managed to fall in with Allan Keith and his party, or it's possible they might have arrived as we should have done, just in time to be too late."

The men belonging to the fort had been successful in extinguishing the flames, though the whole front was either in ruins or presented a fearfully shattered and blackened appearance.

Dr McCrab, with coat off and sleeves tucked up, was busily employed in attending to the wounded men, while Loraine was assisting Sybil and Mrs Mackintosh in calming the fears of poor Effie, who, not seeing Allan Keith among those who had just arrived, had feared that some accident had happened to him. He soon, however, with his active horsemen, having driven the enemy to a distance, arrived unhurt, and his appearance quickly tranquillised her mind.

"We must not, however, forget our friend Mr Harvey," exclaimed Captain Mackintosh. "The Blackfeet may possibly direct their course towards his station and revenge themselves for their failure here by attempting its destruction."

On hearing this remark, Allan Keith and Loraine offered to lead a party of men to the assistance of the missionary, and about thirty of the hunters having volunteered to accompany them, fresh horses were brought across the river, and they immediately set out.

Norman and Hector, notwithstanding their wounds, wished to go, but the Doctor refused to allow them, and insisted on their turning in and getting the rest they greatly needed. Not an hour was lost in commencing the repairs of the fort, that it might be in a condition to resist any further attack which the Indians might venture to make on it. A few men were also sent to bury the Blackfeet, who had fallen either in the attack or flight. Among the bodies that of Mysticoose himself was found, his followers being unable to carry him away. He was buried in the common grave at a distance from the fort.

Of course a watch was kept at night, though it was not thought probable that the Indians, even should they discover the absence of Loraine and Keith, would renew the attack.

A week passed by. The sawyers and carpenters had worked so energetically, that already the fort had assumed its former appearance, with some improvements to add to its strength. There was no time to be lost, as winter was approaching, and most of the men who had arrived under Dan Maloney and Dr McCrab, had to return to Fort Edmonton.

Sybil and Effie had at first kept up their spirits, but they were growing anxious at the non-appearance of Loraine and Keith.

Evening was approaching, when a shout was raised by the sentry on the western watch-tower, that a large train was coming across the prairie, on which Norman and Hector, with several other inmates of the fort, hastened up the platform to take a look at it.

"I am much mistaken, if they are not Loraine and Keith and their party," exclaimed Hector.

"They have carts with them, so there can be no doubt about their being white men," said Norman.

Hector getting a telescope soon discovered that he was right in his conjectures. As the train drew nearer, the gates were opened, and a large party hurried out to meet the newcomers, who proved to be not only those who were expected, but Mr Harvey and his family, with several Indians who had accompanied them.

"He came," he said, "to ask for protection for himself and his wife and children, as well as for the converts, until it could be ascertained that the Blackfeet had finally left the district."

It need not be said that Loraine and Keith had warmly urged him to take this step.

Captain Mackintosh, giving him a hearty welcome, assured him of the use he would be to the inmates of the fort.

"In truth, my dear friend," he observed, "I believe you can do more real good among my half heathen people, than you could to any of the few Indians who would visit you during the winter."

Mr Harvey, besides his wife, had two daughters, nearly grown up, and a son, who, there could be no doubt, would prove a great addition to the society at the fort, the inmates of which had little chance of enjoying much communication with the outer world for many months to come.

Soon after his arrival, Mr Harvey inquired for Isaac Sass. "I half expected to have found him here," he observed to Captain Mackintosh, "though he left without saying in what direction he was going. I am thankful to believe that his visit to me was of spiritual benefit to him; for, opening his heart, he confessed that he had been a careless liver, having endeavoured, though in vain, to put God out of his thoughts. I was the instrument of bringing his mind into a better state, and I trust that in a contrite spirit he sought forgiveness from God through the gracious means He has offered to sinners. Before leaving me, he put into my hands a packet to be delivered to you; and from what he said, I suspect that he is deeply interested in the young lady whom I believed to be your daughter, until he assured me that such was not the case. He had recognised her by her likeness to one whom he truly loved, but who had been lost to him for ever, though, I conclude, you will learn his history from the contents of the packet which I now give you."

Captain Mackintosh, on opening the packet, found it contained a long manuscript written in a large but somewhat shaky hand. It would occupy too much space were it to be copied. His life, like that of many others, had been an adventurous one. His true name was Hugh Lindsay, and his family was an old and good one. Having left home at an early age, he entered the service of the Hudson's Bay Company, and had every reason to expect to become one of its leading members, when his family so strongly expressed their annoyance at hearing of his marriage with a beautiful half-Cree girl, that he ceased to hold any communication with them. He had not long after this quarrelled with his employers, when he left their service, and commenced the life of a free trader and trapper. For some time he had considerable success, and as his wife had presented him with a daughter, whom he devotedly loved, he was doubly anxious to gain the means of supporting and educating her in the rank of a lady. Neither he nor her mother, however, could bear to part with her.

At an early age she was seen and admired by Donald Grey, a young clerk in the service of the Hudson's Bay Company, who sought for and obtained her hand. He, however, had managed, as his father-in-law had done, to quarrel with the chief officer of the fort where he was stationed, and having some means of his own, had taken up his residence at the Red River Settlement.

After living there a year, and becoming the father of a little girl, he received intelligence from England that he had inherited a good property. He had embarked with his young wife and child and a Cree nurse, intending to proceed through the Lake of the Woods, across Lake Superior to Canada. From that day, weeks, months, and years went by, and the old trapper, still supposing that they had arrived safely in England, waited in vain to receive intelligence of them.

It is necessary here to remark that when the superintendent at the company's post on the Sault Saint Marie made inquiries of the chief factors and other officers throughout the north-west territory, they replied that no person connected with them was missing, or had crossed Lake Superior at the time he mentioned. From the American traders also he could obtain no information. Not until Isaac Sass, or more properly, Hugh Lindsay, heard Captain Mackintosh describe the way Sybil had been discovered, did he suspect the fate of his daughter and son-in-law. He had accounted for never having received a letter from them, by supposing that on reaching the old country, and occupying a new sphere of life, they had forgotten him, or had not taken the trouble to write. His wife, dying soon after their daughter's marriage, he had taken to the wild life he had from that time forward led, believing that he himself was forgotten by his kindred, and endeavouring in a misanthropical spirit to banish from his mind all thoughts of the past.

On seeing Sybil, a chord had been struck in his heart, and on hearing her history, he was at once convinced, from her extraordinary likeness to his own child, that she was her daughter though fairer, and of a more refined beauty, such as mental culture gives; but for her sake he was unwilling to make himself known, believing that neither she nor Loraine would be gratified at finding that she was the grand-daughter of a rough old trapper. He especially fancied that the gentlemanly young Englishman would object to him, and having himself a bad opinion of human nature, he supposed that it might even cause him to give up Sybil. Still, after he had been brought to a better state of mind by Mr Harvey, he could not resist the temptation of writing a sketch of his history, and by informing his grand-daughter of her birth and parentage, enable her, as he hoped, to gain the property which would have been her father's. He added all the information he possessed for the discovery of Ronald Grey's family, and whether or not he had ever arrived in England.

While listening to this narrative which Captain Mackintosh read to him, Loraine exclaimed, "Grey was my mother's name, and I remember hearing that a cousin of hers had gone out to the north-west territory, in the service of the Hudson's Bay Company, and that although property had been left him he had not returned to claim it, and has never since been heard of. Ultimately it came to my mother, through whom it forms a portion of the fortune I possess, and I will willingly resign it to the rightful heiress."

"I don't suppose that she, with equal willingness, will deprive you of it," said Captain Mackintosh, laughing.

Mr Harvey again expressed his regret that the old man had not remained behind with him, though he added, "I felt confident he has embraced the truth as it is in Christ Jesus, and I fully expect to see him again before long."

The wounded men having recovered under the care of Dr McCrab, he and Dan Maloney returned, with a portion of their followers, to Fort Edmonton, while the half-breeds set off eastward for their homes at the Red River. Allan Keith, much to his own satisfaction, having had permission to remain at Fort Duncan with the rest, to reinforce its garrison.

It was fully expected that the old trapper would some day make his appearance, but time went by, and no tidings could be gained of him.

Before Mr Harvey returned in the spring to his mission station, he united Sybil and Effie to the two gentlemen to whom they had given their hearts.

Loraine and his bride immediately set off for the Red River, intending to proceed from thence to Canada, on their way to England, while Allan Keith took his to a fort, to the charge of which he had been appointed.

Loraine, by means of the information Captain Mackintosh had given him, and such as he was able to obtain at the Red River, was able to prove that his wife was the daughter of Ronald Grey, but was saved a vast amount of legal expenses by her refusal to claim the property of which he was already in possession.

Some time afterwards, Allan Keith and Effie came over to pay them a visit. They brought some deeply interesting information. Search had for a long time been fruitlessly made for the old hunter, until at length, Norman and Hector Mackintosh, when on an exploring expedition, had discovered on a tree-covered hill, overlooking a calm lake, a solitary grave. Over it had been placed, in regular order, a pile of huge logs, cut by an Indian axe. Searching further, they found in a hut hard by, a hump-backed Indian, life apparently ebbing fast away.

He pointed above. "I am going," he whispered, "to that heaven of which my friend and protector, he who lies yonder, has told me, through the merits of One who died for sinful men. I have fulfilled his last wish, which was to be buried, and but yesterday finished my task. It has been a long one, for the trees were hard to cut down, and now I go with joy to meet him, in the happy land from which there is no return. I am thankful that you have come to know where he is laid."

In the hopes of resuscitating the poor lad, Norman and Hector endeavoured to make him take some nourishment, but he was in too exhausted a condition to swallow the food, and he breathed his last just as the setting sun cast a bright glow across the calm waters on the old trapper's grave.

ABOUT THE AUTHOR

William Henry Giles Kingston (1814 - 1880), writer of tales for boys, born in London, but spent much of his youth in Oporto, where his father was a merchant.

His first book, The Circassian Chief, appeared in 1844. His first book for boys, Peter the Whaler, was published in 1851, and had such success that he retired from business and devoted himself entirely to the production of this kind of literature, in which his popularity was deservedly great; and during 30 years he wrote upwards of 130 tales, including The Three Midshipmen (1862), The Three Lieutenants (1874), The Three Commanders (1875), The Three Admirals (1877), Digby Heathcote, etc.

He also conducted various papers, including The Colonist, and Colonial Magazine and East India Review. He was also interested in emigration, volunteering, and various philanthropic schemes. For services in negotiating a commercial treaty with Portugal he received a Portuguese knighthood, and for his literary labours a Government pension.

Choose from Thousands of 1stWorldLibrary Classics By

A. M. Barnard
Ada Leverson
Adolphus William Ward
Aesop
Agatha Christie
Alexander Aaronsohn
Alexander Kielland
Alexandre Dumas
Alfred Gatty
Alfred Ollivant
Alice Duer Miller
Alice Turner Curtis
Alice Dunbar
Allen Chapman
Alleyne Ireland
Ambrose Bierce
Amelia E. Barr
Amory H. Bradford
Andrew Lang
Andrew McFarland Davis
Andy Adams
Angela Brazil
Anna Alice Chapin
Anna Sewell
Annie Besant
Annie Hamilton Donnell
Annie Payson Call
Annie Roe Carr
Annonaymous
Anton Chekhov
Archibald Lee Fletcher
Arnold Bennett
Arthur C. Benson
Arthur Conan Doyle
Arthur M. Winfield
Arthur Ransome
Arthur Schnitzler
Arthur Train
Atticus
B.H. Baden-Powell
B. M. Bower
B. C. Chatterjee
Baroness Emmuska Orczy
Baroness Orczy
Basil King
Bayard Taylor
Ben Macomber
Bertha Muzzy Bower
Bjornstjerne Bjornson

Booth Tarkington
Boyd Cable
Bram Stoker
C. Collodi
C. E. Orr
C. M. Ingleby
Carolyn Wells
Catherine Parr Traill
Charles A. Eastman
Charles Amory Beach
Charles Dickens
Charles Dudley Warner
Charles Farrar Browne
Charles Ives
Charles Kingsley
Charles Klein
Charles Hanson Towne
Charles Lathrop Pack
Charles Romyn Dake
Charles Whibley
Charles Willing Beale
Charlotte M. Braeme
Charlotte M. Yonge
Charlotte Perkins Stetson
Clair W. Hayes
Clarence Day Jr.
Clarence E. Mulford
Clemence Housman
Confucius
Coningsby Dawson
Cornelis DeWitt Wilcox
Cyril Burleigh
D. H. Lawrence
Daniel Defoe
David Garnett
Dinah Craik
Don Carlos Janes
Donald Keyhoe
Dorothy Kilner
Dougan Clark
Douglas Fairbanks
E. Nesbit
E. P. Roe
E. Phillips Oppenheim
E. S. Brooks
Earl Barnes
Edgar Rice Burroughs
Edith Van Dyne
Edith Wharton

Edward Everett Hale
Edward J. O'Biren
Edward S. Ellis
Edwin L. Arnold
Eleanor Atkins
Eleanor Hallowell Abbott
Eliot Gregory
Elizabeth Gaskell
Elizabeth McCracken
Elizabeth Von Arnim
Ellem Key
Emerson Hough
Emilie F. Carlen
Emily Bronte
Emily Dickinson
Enid Bagnold
Enilor Macartney Lane
Erasmus W. Jones
Ernie Howard Pie
Ethel May Dell
Ethel Turner
Ethel Watts Mumford
Eugene Sue
Eugenie Foa
Eugene Wood
Eustace Hale Ball
Evelyn Everett-green
Everard Cotes
F. H. Cheley
F. J. Cross
F. Marion Crawford
Fannie E. Newberry
Federick Austin Ogg
Ferdinand Ossendowski
Fergus Hume
Florence A. Kilpatrick
Fremont B. Deering
Francis Bacon
Francis Darwin
Frances Hodgson Burnett
Frances Parkinson Keyes
Frank Gee Patchin
Frank Harris
Frank Jewett Mather
Frank L. Packard
Frank V. Webster
Frederic Stewart Isham
Frederick Trevor Hill
Frederick Winslow Taylor

Friedrich Kerst
Friedrich Nietzsche
Fyodor Dostoyevsky
G.A. Henty
G.K. Chesterton
Gabrielle E. Jackson
Garrett P. Serviss
Gaston Leroux
George A. Warren
George Ade
Geroge Bernard Shaw
George Cary Eggleston
George Durston
George Ebers
George Eliot
George Gissing
George MacDonald
George Meredith
George Orwell
George Sylvester Viereck
George Tucker
George W. Cable
George Wharton James
Gertrude Atherton
Gordon Casserly
Grace E. King
Grace Gallatin
Grace Greenwood
Grant Allen
Guillermo A. Sherwell
Gulielma Zollinger
Gustav Flaubert
H. A. Cody
H. B. Irving
H.C. Bailey
H. G. Wells
H. H. Munro
H. Irving Hancock
H. R. Naylor
H. Rider Haggard
H. W. C. Davis
Haldeman Julius
Hall Caine
Hamilton Wright Mabie
Hans Christian Andersen
Harold Avery
Harold McGrath
Harriet Beecher Stowe
Harry Castlemon
Harry Coghill
Harry Houidini

Hayden Carruth
Helent Hunt Jackson
Helen Nicolay
Hendrik Conscience
Hendy David Thoreau
Henri Barbusse
Henrik Ibsen
Henry Adams
Henry Ford
Henry Frost
Henry James
Henry Jones Ford
Henry Seton Merriman
Henry W Longfellow
Herbert A. Giles
Herbert Carter
Herbert N. Casson
Herman Hesse
Hildegard G. Frey
Homer
Honore De Balzac
Horace B. Day
Horace Walpole
Horatio Alger Jr.
Howard Pyle
Howard R. Garis
Hugh Lofting
Hugh Walpole
Humphry Ward
Ian Maclaren
Inez Haynes Gillmore
Irving Bacheller
Isabel Cecilia Williams
Isabel Hornibrook
Israel Abrahams
Ivan Turgenev
J.G.Austin
J. Henri Fabre
J. M. Barrie
J. M. Walsh
J. Macdonald Oxley
J. R. Miller
J. S. Fletcher
J. S. Knowles
J. Storer Clouston
J. W. Duffield
Jack London
Jacob Abbott
James Allen
James Andrews
James Baldwin

James Branch Cabell
James DeMille
James Joyce
James Lane Allen
James Lane Allen
James Oliver Curwood
James Oppenheim
James Otis
James R. Driscoll
Jane Abbott
Jane Austen
Jane L. Stewart
Janet Aldridge
Jens Peter Jacobsen
Jerome K. Jerome
Jessie Graham Flower
John Buchan
John Burroughs
John Cournos
John F. Kennedy
John Gay
John Glasworthy
John Habberton
John Joy Bell
John Kendrick Bangs
John Milton
John Philip Sousa
John Taintor Foote
Jonas Lauritz Idemil Lie
Jonathan Swift
Joseph A. Altsheler
Joseph Carey
Joseph Conrad
Joseph E. Badger Jr
Joseph Hergesheimer
Joseph Jacobs
Jules Vernes
Julian Hawthrone
Julie A Lippmann
Justin Huntly McCarthy
Kakuzo Okakura
Karle Wilson Baker
Kate Chopin
Kenneth Grahame
Kenneth McGaffey
Kate Langley Bosher
Kate Langley Bosher
Katherine Cecil Thurston
Katherine Stokes
L. A. Abbot
L. T. Meade

L. Frank Baum
Latta Griswold
Laura Dent Crane
Laura Lee Hope
Laurence Housman
Lawrence Beasley
Leo Tolstoy
Leonid Andreyev
Lewis Carroll
Lewis Sperry Chafer
Lilian Bell
Lloyd Osbourne
Louis Hughes
Louis Joseph Vance
Louis Tracy
Louisa May Alcott
Lucy Fitch Perkins
Lucy Maud Montgomery
Luther Benson
Lydia Miller Middleton
Lyndon Orr
M. Corvus
M. H. Adams
Margaret E. Sangster
Margret Howth
Margaret Vandercook
Margaret W. Hungerford
Margret Penrose
Maria Edgeworth
Maria Thompson Daviess
Mariano Azuela
Marion Polk Angellotti
Mark Overton
Mark Twain
Mary Austin
Mary Catherine Crowley
Mary Cole
Mary Hastings Bradley
Mary Roberts Rinehart
Mary Rowlandson
M. Wollstonecraft Shelley
Maud Lindsay
Max Beerbohm
Myra Kelly
Nathaniel Hawthrone
Nicolo Machiavelli
O. F. Walton
Oscar Wilde

Owen Johnson
P.G. Wodehouse
Paul and Mabel Thorne
Paul G. Tomlinson
Paul Severing
Percy Brebner
Percy Keese Fitzhugh
Peter B. Kyne
Plato
Quincy Allen
R. Derby Holmes
R. L. Stevenson
R. S. Ball
Rabindranath Tagore
Rahul Alvares
Ralph Bonehill
Ralph Henry Barbour
Ralph Victor
Ralph Waldo Emmerson
Rene Descartes
Ray Cummings
Rex Beach
Rex E. Beach
Richard Harding Davis
Richard Jefferies
Richard Le Gallienne
Robert Barr
Robert Frost
Robert Gordon Anderson
Robert L. Drake
Robert Lansing
Robert Lynd
Robert Michael Ballantyne
Robert W. Chambers
Rosa Nouchette Carey
Rudyard Kipling
Saint Augustine
Samuel B. Allison
Samuel Hopkins Adams
Sarah Bernhardt
Sarah C. Hallowell
Selma Lagerlof
Sherwood Anderson
Sigmund Freud
Standish O'Grady
Stanley Weyman
Stella Benson
Stella M. Francis

Stephen Crane
Stewart Edward White
Stijn Streuvels
Swami Abhedananda
Swami Parmananda
T. S. Ackland
T. S. Arthur
The Princess Der Ling
Thomas A. Janvier
Thomas A Kempis
Thomas Anderton
Thomas Bailey Aldrich
Thomas Bulfinch
Thomas De Quincey
Thomas Dixon
Thomas H. Huxley
Thomas Hardy
Thomas More
Thornton W. Burgess
U. S. Grant
Upton Sinclair
Valentine Williams
Various Authors
Vaughan Kester
Victor Appleton
Victor G. Durham
Victoria Cross
Virginia Woolf
Wadsworth Camp
Walter Camp
Walter Scott
Washington Irving
Wilbur Lawton
Wilkie Collins
Willa Cather
Willard F. Baker
William Dean Howells
William le Queux
W. Makepeace Thackeray
William W. Walter
William Shakespeare
Winston Churchill
Yei Theodora Ozaki
Yogi Ramacharaka
Young E. Allison
Zane Grey